BREA
HASTE

Finding God in Ordinary Life

REBECCA & JAY MADDEN

©2023 by Jay and Rebecca Madden

Published by hope*books
2217 Matthews Township Pkwy
Suite D302
Matthews, NC 28105
www.hopebooks.com

hope*books is a division of hope*media

Printed in the United States of America by hope*books

All rights reserved. Without limiting the rights under copyrights reserved above, no part of this publication may be scanned, uploaded, reproduced, distributed, or transmitted in any form or by any means whatsoever without express prior written permission from both the author and publisher of this book—except in the case of brief quotations embodied in critical articles and reviews.

Thank you for supporting the author's rights.

First paperback edition.
Paperback ISBN: 979-8-89185-008-8
Hardcover ISBN: 979-8-89185-017-0
Ebook ISBN: 979-8-89185-009-5
Library of Congress Number: 2023920329

Cover image by Victor Lacey

Unless otherwise indicated, all Scripture quotations taken from The Holy Bible, New International Version® (NIV)® Copyright © 1973, 1978, 1984, 2011 by Biblica, Inc. Used by permission.

*To "Hatsy" Young, Rebecca's mother,
who at the age of ninety-seven suggested that we write this book.*

*May these written words bring you joy in heaven, and may
it also bring delight to the rest of the great cloud of witnesses.*

I will stand at my post,

I will take up my position on the watch-tower,

I will watch to learn what [God] will say through me,

and what I shall reply when I am challenged.

Then the L<small>ORD</small> *made answer:*

Write down the vision, inscribe it on tablets,

ready for a herald to carry it with speed;

for there is still a vision for the appointed time.

At the destined hour it will come in **breathless haste,**

it will not fail.

If it delays, wait for it;

for when it comes will be no time to linger.

The reckless will be unsure of himself,

while the righteous one will live by being faithful . . .

H<small>ABAKKUK</small> 2:1–4, <small>NEB</small> (emphasis added)

ENDORSEMENTS

Like the book of Esther from the Bible, sometimes God's presence is most known through the weaving together of our story. What begins as ordinary love and tragedy for Rebecca and Jay turns into beautiful redemption. Your story will be enriched by reading theirs.

Dr. Richard Kannwischer
Senior Pastor, Peachtree Presbyterian Church Atlanta, GA

Breathless Haste reminds us that even in those moments that we are frantically racing through life, or are scared, God is always there, always steady. Through frank, page-turning stories, Rebecca and Jay Madden share crushing moments of loss and those of jubilant wonder. Read this book for the epic reminder that God walks along with us, and that by "praying for the extraordinary" and intentionally listening for his voice, He will craft these experiences to help us sing a new song.

Dr. Darria Long
National Bestselling Author of Mom Hacks, national TV health contributor, Emergency physician, and mom of 3

Dallas Willard has suggested that the social dimension of a spiritually-mature person is characterized by transparency, and that is exactly what you'll find in the stories of this book. Each is written with raw, unvarnished, and hope-filled honesty. I applaud Rebecca and Jay for putting so many of their life experiences in story form. You will learn from them about the ongoing dynamic of God's grace in their lives and how, as Dallas also famously said, it is possible to grow in grace.

Gary W. Moon, M.Div., Ph.D.
Founding Executive Director Martin Institute and Dallas Willard Center, Westmont College, Director of Conversatio Divina and Author of Apprenticeship with Jesus, and Becoming Dallas Willard

I never knew that the words heartbreaking, funny, and joy could all go in the same sentence. I love how Rebecca and Jay brought me along their journey. Along with making me cry, laugh and find hope, it was fun to read. This is a must read!

Maina Mwaura
Minister/Journalist
Author of How the life and legacy of Howard Hendricks, Equipped and Inspired a Generation of Leaders

Rebecca and Jay have invited us to read their story and listen to their journey of rediscovering God in the midst of a young marriage, work, loss, and the stress of keeping it all together. This is an invitation that you want to reply YES to. It is a compelling story about a way that God works for good in all things. Join them in making meaning and purpose in your unique story.

Sibyl Towner
Co-director Springs Retreat Center, co-author of
Listen to My Life, and Spiritual Director

This poignant survival guide reminds us how God forms extraordinary faith through ordinary lives. These hard-won lessons will be a path to sustain you through your own loss and longings.

Katherine Wolf
Author of Hope Heals and Suffer Strong, co-founder of Hope Heals ministry

CONTENTS

Introduction (Rebecca) ix

Chapter One: A McDonald's, a Mexican Restaurant, and a
    Superficial Choice (Jay) 1

Chapter Two: An Ocean, a Billboard, and a Miracle (Rebecca) 13

Chapter Three: A Prayer, a Sense of Desperation, and a Cassette Tape (Jay) 33

Chapter Four: A Clock, a Song, and a Mortgage (Rebecca) 45

Chapter Five: Jenga, a Tree, and a Mentor (Jay) 61

Chapter Six: A Speaker, a Meeting, and a Padfolio (Rebecca) 73

Chapter Seven: A Monet Painting, a Bombing, and a Dangerous Trip (Jay) 89

Chapter Eight: A Little Boy, Breathless Haste, and a Scrapbook (Rebecca) 101

Chapter Nine: A Poem, a Phone Call, and a Baby Bonnet (Jay) 115

Chapter Ten: A Neighbor, Dallas Willard, and Bankruptcy (Rebecca) 129

Epilogue: Participation, Posture, and Preparation (Jay) 145

INTRODUCTION

(Rebecca)

For about a decade, I felt a tug at my heart to write this book. Along the way, that idea was confirmed by friends and strangers in countless ways, as they encouraged me to document the stories they had heard or witnessed.

In 2020, I was visiting my ninety-seven-year-old mother. Because of her limited eyesight, she enjoyed having family read to her. On one particular day, she indicated interest in hearing some of the initial chapters I had written for this book. So I climbed into the bed with her and began to read aloud. She listened for a while and then asked if Jay was writing down his stories. When I told her he wasn't, she strongly suggested he should.

Jay was taken aback by this idea. He was hesitant to begin writing again, as he had recently finished writing his doctoral dissertation. After much back-and-forth discussion over the course of a few weeks, Jay decided to join the effort.

For more than twenty years, Jay and I have written in personal journals, documenting our daily lives in the form of scribbled notes with all the questions, affirmations, concerns, struggles, joys, and heartaches we have experienced. Our history and the details written on those pages, along with the words written from our hearts as we reflected on our journey, have provided the content for this spiritual memoir. As we wrote the chapters you are about to read, we shed many tears, awestruck by all the specific ways we found God at work in and through our ordinary lives.

The stories you will encounter in these pages are the highlights and lowlights of how Jay and I experienced God's presence, movement, and direction in our lives. It all began with the tragic loss of our firstborn son and the miraculous healing of our daughter. We have journeyed through unusual circumstances and met people whom God clearly placed on our path. We have been impacted and guided by God through the relationships we have formed, books we read, Scripture that jumped off the pages of our Bibles, revelations we received in nature, prayers unanswered and answered, and His still, small voice.

The chapter titles serve as thirty signposts; each marks a significant experience in which we found God. Scattered throughout the book, you will notice quotations taken directly from our journals, written in the margins. Our hope and prayer is that our words and stories will inspire you to open your eyes and your heart to all the ways you can find God's presence in your own life.

If you would like to continue to read about our experiences of finding God, beyond what we have recorded in this book, follow us at https://www.breathlesshaste.com.

Blessings! Rebecca

CHAPTER ONE

A McDonald's, a Mexican Restaurant, and a Superficial Choice (Jay)

> *When you pass through the waters, I will be with you; and when you pass through the rivers, they will not sweep over you. When you walk through the fire, you will not be burned; the flames will not set you ablaze.*
>
> —Isaiah 43:2

A McDonald's

When we imagine the kind of places where we might find God, what most often comes to mind is a stunning scene on a mountaintop, a walk beside the ocean, or even sitting in a beautiful cathedral. We don't expect to encounter Him in the ordinary places in our lives, but on this day, we did.

We were halfway through the four-and-a-half-hour drive from our home in Greenville, South Carolina, to Birmingham, Alabama, with our six-month-old son, Brock, and we had stopped for a break. Rebecca is a connoisseur of Diet Coke; she insists it's best when dispensed from the fountains of specific fast-food establishments, so we had stopped at a McDonald's. While Rebecca stood in line, she struck up a conversation with a mother who was there with her child. Rebecca asked how old the woman's son was, and the woman responded that he was eleven months old. Rebecca told the woman that we had a son who was six months old, and then she blurted out that we were taking him to Birmingham for heart surgery.

This woman, a complete stranger, replied, "My son has tetralogy of Fallot. He was operated on when he was six months old."

In a state of disbelief, Rebecca shared that this was Brock's condition as well.

The woman said, "Don't let anyone tell you that there won't be complications, because there will be." She went on to say that the recovery period had been horrible, but they had been able to go home two weeks after surgery. She wished us well, and they went on their way.

We climbed back into the car, buckled our seatbelts, and continued on our journey to Birmingham, grappling with the meaning of this surprising encounter.

Our doctors informed us that approximately 1 percent of newborns have congenital heart defects. About 10 percent of those have tetralogy of Fallot, so the fact that we were together in a line at this McDonald's at this time on this day was astonishing. We were convinced that this was a "God moment." It gave us encouragement, and in retrospect, it presented us with clear evidence that God knew exactly where we were and what was ahead. It was a sign of His presence, and it gave us hope that everything would work out in the end, just as it had for that family. It was the latest in a long line of faith-building moments that had begun with Brock's birth.

Chapter One

In the fall of 1992, we were excited to find out that we were expecting our first child. However, a few weeks into the pregnancy, Rebecca began to bleed and had to go to the emergency room. We were on pins and needles for several weeks, but an ultrasound eventually revealed a strong heartbeat. The baby seemed fine. This was a huge relief, and the rest of the pregnancy proceeded normally. On August 7, 1993, after Rebecca had labored for thirty painful hours, Henry Brockington Madden was born. As he was delivered, I noticed the nurses exchanging looks with one another. We soon learned that he was missing most of his outer left ear. This, of course, was very concerning for us, and it set off internal alarm bells for the medical staff. The medical team knew that this abnormality could indicate a wide spectrum of other congenital conditions. They made the decision to transfer him to another hospital's NICU for further tests.

Rebecca had to wait for twenty-four hours before she could be discharged from the hospital where she had delivered, so we made the decision that I would go with Brock. We were exhausted, in shock, and deeply concerned about what was ahead. At times like this, a person's mind becomes filled with all kinds of horrible scenarios. I vividly remember going outside into a hospital courtyard to pray and try to collect myself. My first thought was to tell God, "You are not going to push me away with this." I recognize the strangeness of this response, but it felt as if God was trying to distance Himself from me, to reject me or abandon me, and that this was His method. It would take a lot of work down the road to understand the source of that impulse, but at that moment I was just trying to hang on to my faith in the midst of what felt like yet another unanswered prayer.

Just a few years prior to this, my father had died at age fifty-two after a terrible six-month battle with cancer, and I had also lost my maternal grandfather, whom I had loved deeply. Would I now lose my son? It seemed to me that God was not answering my prayers to protect the ones I loved—at the least, he hadn't answered in the ways I had hoped He would. I thought my faith was solid, but time and time again, things continued to turn out badly. Despite my hopes and prayers, I continued to experience loss and tragedy. I believed that God was real, but he seemed distant, uninterested in these tragedies in my life. Or I thought that maybe, for some reason, He was trying to push me further away.

Soon after Brock was born, Rebecca and I met with a doctor who sat down with a legal pad and shared the potential issues with Brock. Each item on his list was another blow to our exhausted minds and hearts. Eventually, most of the tests revealed nothing wrong. However, before we left the hospital, a cardiologist discovered a congenital heart defect called tetralogy of Fallot, which involves a combination of four heart defects and affects the flow of oxygenated blood in the body. We were told that he would need surgery to correct the heart defect, but that it could wait for a year or two. We went home concerned, but relieved that the legal pad full of possibilities had not been true.

As the weeks passed, Brock thrived. When he was just a few weeks old, we visited his grandparents in Florence, South Carolina. While there, Rebecca read an article in the local newspaper titled "Vanishing Twin Could Cause Birth Defects." The article explained how when one identical twin is miscarried, it can damage the survivor and interfere with their development. Rebecca was convinced that this was what had happened early in her pregnancy, when she ended up in the emergency room in December with bleeding. She was struck by the timing of

Chapter One

seeing and reading this article in her hometown newspaper during our brief visit. I think when dealing with situations like this, we look for something to make some sense of it. For Rebecca, this article—and the perfect timing of when she found it—helped.

We began to do research on Brock's ear defect, and we met with a plastic surgeon in Atlanta who specialized in ear reconstruction for children. I remember having our family picture taken for the church directory during that time. While we were waiting our turn with the photographer, a child noticed Brock's ear and asked her mother what was wrong with him. It was a painful moment for me, as I imagined this scenario being played out again and again in the years ahead. We were looking forward to being able to have his ear reconstructed.

We also began to research his heart condition, and we learned that most of the best hospitals and surgeons were recommending surgery for tetralogy of Fallot before six months of age. After much prayer, research, and a visit with the surgeon, we decided to have the surgery done at the University of Alabama at Birmingham Hospital on February 7, 1993.

That day began as expected, a seemingly routine and successful open-heart surgery. After a long day of waiting and worrying, we went back to our hotel to rest. We were awakened that night by the phone ringing beside our bed. We were told that Brock's condition was deteriorating. He needed to go back into surgery, so the doctors could try to determine the source of the problem.

Being awakened by that call is seared into my memory. In fact, even all these years later, I can't sleep with a phone beside my bed unless it is turned off or the ringer is disabled. That call marked the beginning of a seven-day nightmare that included Brock going back into surgery two more times. In the end, he never woke up. For whatever reason, the routine operation was too much for his little body, and he passed away on Valentine's Day, 1993. Before we left him, Rebecca held him one more time. I can clearly remember the scene of her holding him in the hospital room; the shades were pulled down, and I could see sunlight peeking in around the edges of the windows. She remembers I declined that chance to hold him. Back then, my approach to grief was to get away from it as quickly as possible.

During our darkest days of sorrow, we often referred back to our encounter at McDonald's. The other mom had told us that there would be complications. Was this what she meant? She had eventually brought her son home, so we had thought that would be the way it would go for us. However, our story took a very different and heartbreaking turn. With many years of hindsight, I am still convinced that we encountered God's presence in that conversation. But it was not so much God signaling our destination, it was Him letting us know that He saw us, He knew our struggles, and He would be with us through it all.

The weeks and months following Brock's death seemed like a distant darkness that we somehow passed. The loss of a child is an unnatural experience. We instinctively know that this is not how life is supposed to be. Although I had recently suffered the loss of beloved family members, this was different. I was left with the feeling that a part of me had died and that part would always be missing. We endured a large funeral and a graveside service during which Brock was placed in a mausoleum next to my father. These gatherings were followed by a lunch in our home, surrounded by friends and family, as per Southern tradition.

It was our faith community that carried us through that time. It was the church that provided a place for us to grieve and to experience the love of friends, and it was the church that eventually helped us to move forward with our lives. We had both grown up in Christian homes and attended Baptist churches. I sometimes joke that we are recovering Southern Baptists. However, the truth is that those

> "One of the major reasons we were able to cope is because of the love and support of our church."
>
> April 27, 1997

churches were the special places where we first heard the gospel, believed, and were baptized, all of which laid a strong foundation for what was to come.

Before Rebecca and I had even met, God was preparing us through our church backgrounds. When we went away to college, each of us conveniently put our faith up on a shelf. We didn't reject faith, we just put it away, sort of like a trust fund. We knew that God loved us, and He was there if we needed him. Obviously, we had a limited perspective of what it meant to follow Jesus. Like so many of our generation, for us, the gospel was primarily about accepting Jesus so we could go to heaven. After that, we thought all we had to do was stay out of trouble and follow the rules. In the years ahead, we would learn that there was much more to following Jesus than simply being good, but it was our early church experiences that ignited the flame. At times that flame may have been weak, but it was never extinguished.

A Mexican Restaurant

Rebecca and I never met during our college years, which was probably lucky for me. After Rebecca graduated from Clemson, she began working for IBM in Greenville, where I returned home after college and a stint in the Army. It was there that God wove our stories together in a Mexican restaurant, of all places. Rebecca lived in an apartment complex across the street from this restaurant, and a friend of mine also lived in her complex. He asked me to go to a meet-your-neighbor party at the restaurant with him, assuring me that there would be lots of girls in attendance. I agreed to go, never imagining that for me, it would be a meet-your-wife party. Our group ended up at a table with Rebecca's group. We talked quite a bit that night and seemed to connect, so I asked her out for lunch. And thus, it began. A few days later, we realized that a mutual friend had previously attempted to set us up. I had not wanted to go on a blind date. I guess God decided that if He could not get me out on a blind date, He could always get me to a Mexican restaurant.

During our first few months of dating, my father was diagnosed with inoperable lung cancer. I was an only child, and I was working with him in his business. The six-month period between his diagnosis and death was a horrible time for me. Watching a parent waste away and not being able to change the situation is a painful and frustrating experience. My father, whom I loved very much, was a workaholic. He worked seven days a week building his business so he could achieve his dream of retiring at the beach. As a result, I felt as if we were never able to spend enough time together. Most of my childhood memories with him are of me tagging along with him to work. These experiences carried over into adulthood, impacting my decisions about my work, my approach to fatherhood, and even my view of God. In fact, as I reflected later, my decision to leave the Army and go into the family business was not based on a passion for that business or a dislike for the Army, as I actually thrived in that environment. I came home to the family business for one simple reason: my dad asked me to. Deep down, I was still a little boy wanting to spend time with his father.

Chapter One

Losing my father after such a short period of time working together was a bitter pill to swallow. But during those months of his illness, one thing became clear. My fun date from the Mexican restaurant was someone special. She was there at my side through all the pain of losing my dad, when it would have been much easier to slip away. His illness had quickly taken our relationship from light and fun to grim and hard. It made me realize that she was a person who could be counted on. We could get through hard times together, the kind of times that can either draw two people closer or tear them apart. In retrospect, I guess that this was a stress test for what was to come.

A Superficial Choice

Losing a child is excruciating. The initial grief is a crushing pain, followed by long months of walking through each day as if in a fog. Everything feels heavier, and it can strain your closest relationships, even the ones with your spouse and with God. Rebecca and I soon discovered that we approached grief very differently. I had more experience with loss, but this experience seemingly had taught me very little. When I felt sad, my inclination was not to discuss it, but to go into my shell instead. I wanted to pull the covers over my head and be alone. The last thing I wanted to do was to lean into the pain of my emotions or to weep, even with Rebecca. I did what I always had done: stuff it and keep trying to move forward. I was outwardly coping, but inwardly dying.

Rebecca had less experience with grief, but she had a much healthier approach. She wanted to talk about it. She needed to talk about it. I can remember her saying, "You never want to talk about it," and me retorting, "It's *all* you want to talk about." As the months passed, we discovered that our disconnect over grieving was sometimes a matter of timing. We just didn't grieve on the same schedule. There would be times when Rebecca was feeling better, and I would be in a funk. It would then reverse itself, leaving us to wonder how one of us could be in a good mood when the other was so sad. The death of a child puts a severe strain on a marriage and can drive a wedge between the parents.

> "The only thing worse than being separated from my son would be being separated from Christ. My only chance to see my son again is the eternal life offered by Christ."
>
> *Spring 1994*

Thankfully, we never drifted apart. Through God's grace we hung on to one another, accepting that even though we grieved in different ways, we could walk through it together.

When you suffer deep pain, it either draws you closer to God, or you push Him away. It hurts too much to stay in the same place spiritually. In retrospect, losing Brock was a part of us drawing closer to God. To be clear, that is not why we lost him, but it did result in us digging deep into the faith we had so conveniently put on shelves in college. Our church was a large part of that growth. After we were married and had begun to think about starting a family, we decided we needed to find a community of faith. In truth, this was probably the Spirit drawing us back to God for what was to come. It would be nice to describe our choice of First Presbyterian Church as a deeply prayed over and theologically grounded decision, but the truth is that we made a superficial choice. With its architecture and stained-glass windows, the church was beautiful, and we were drawn to that beauty. It was also located near our house, and the people seemed nice. God uses many ways to lead us, even ways that appear superficial.

The church community we became a part of at First Presbyterian was a Sunday school class called the Flock. The Flock was a large group

Chapter One

of young couples in a similar stage of life. They were starting families, building careers, and trying to integrate life with faith. After Brock's death, those friends gave us the love and support we so desperately needed. We experienced Jesus through their words and prayers and through the meals they delivered—actions that helped us to believe that all of this was somehow in God's plan. In essence, God loved us through them by providing a picture of Christian community, a picture that continues to inspire us in our life and ministry. Some of our best friendships began there and have remained strong all these decades later, despite the many miles and years that have separated us. We bonded through our tragedy and their love for us.

That kind of love is really what is most needed by those experiencing grief. In my role as a pastor, people often tell me that they don't know what to say to someone who has suffered a tragedy. My advice is simply to say that you love them. More often than not, many of the other things that are said will sound inadequate at best and hurtful at worst. Not long after we lost Brock, a man told Rebecca that he understood our grief because he had just lost a pet. I, too, have cried when one of my dogs has died, so I recognize that grief. But I don't recommend making that comparison to a grieving mother.

In times of great sorrow, you may also hear quite a bit of Christian pep talk, such as, "God is in control" or "God is good all the time." It seems that many of us feel the need to defend God's character by reminding suffering people of His goodness. That approach is not helpful to God or to those who are suffering. Deep pain and tragedy are not easily explained away. The *why* question is unanswerable and can eat away at a person's soul and ability to move forward. The truth is that even if we knew why something horrible had happened, it wouldn't change the fact that it was horrible.

Following Brock's death, I was slowly learning that it's okay to be sad, confused, and angry. Scripture is filled with the outpouring of authentic emotion. We experience the presence of God when we "pass through the waters" and "walk through the fire" (Isaiah 43:2), not by rationalizing our loss or papering over it, but by sitting in it. We only have to read about Jesus's reaction to the death of Lazarus (John 11:1-44) to see that pain and grief are part of the process of being fully human. I was slowly learning that my way of coping with loss was unhealthy for me, my faith, and those I love. I needed to gain the capacity to grieve in a healthy way. It was necessary for my healing and for finding God in the ordinary and in the miraculous.

FOR REFLECTION

Take a few minutes to journal in response to these questions:

- ▶ What has been your greatest loss? How did you experience God's presence during that time?
- ▶ Would you describe your faith as active? Or do you have it on the shelf for a rainy day?
- ▶ How do you typically process grief or difficult times in your life? Do you think your approach is healthy? Why, or why not?
- ▶ What has been your richest experience with community? What made it so meaningful?

CHAPTER TWO

An Ocean, a Billboard, and a Miracle (Rebecca)

> *Now to him who is able to do immeasurably more than all we ask or imagine, according to his power that is at work within us to him be glory in the church and in Christ Jesus throughout all generations, for ever and ever! Amen.*
>
> —Ephesians 3:20–21

Up until the time Brock was born, I thought I was the one in control of my life—in control of my job, money, family, and marriage. And my faith wasn't intertwined with any of that. However, when it was time for Brock's surgery, it became clear that both my life and his life were totally out of my control. I prayed more that week than I had likely prayed in my whole life, but those prayers were not answered in the way I had hoped.

Somewhere in my fog of grief shortly after Brock's death, God carved these words into my heart: there is a heaven. I'm not sure how it happened. It wasn't an audible voice, nor was it a still, small voice. I can only describe it as a very deep impression. Certainly, most of my life I would have told you that I thought that heaven existed. However, when you experience death so closely and personally, your life and beliefs are turned upside down. Instead of turning away from God, I decided to fully bet my life on this idea of heaven, and I placed my faith and life in the hands of the One who created the heaven I couldn't see and the earth I could. What did I have to lose? As I grieved my loss, this anchor kept me from checking myself into an insane asylum.

In January 1995, not quite a year after Brock's death, I found out that I was expecting again. Doctors told us that a child who has a sibling with a heart defect has a 4–13 percent chance of being born with one too. The doctor recommended having Level 2 ultrasounds regularly during the pregnancy to get a better and more detailed look at the baby's development and ensure everything was fine. The early ultrasound revealed that the baby was a girl and that she was developing normally. We were thankful and relieved, but an underlying anxiousness was still present.

We named her Neale Covington after my great-aunt who left her small town of Florence, South Carolina, as a young woman to become a missionary in Nigeria. She served from 1920 to 1961. We loved that our daughter would share the name of a strong, fearless, and courageous Christian woman. A few months later, we went back for another ultrasound as part of monitoring Neale throughout her fetal development. This study revealed that the left side of Neale's heart was smaller than the right side. The fetal/pediatric cardiologist explained that the left side of the heart was the pumping chamber for the heart and that it was normally larger than the right side. Neale's heart measured in the 5th percentile on the left, while the right side measured in the 95th

Chapter Two

percentile. This large discrepancy indicated a diagnosis of a hypoplastic left heart. The cardiologist also noticed an aortic coarctation, which is a narrowing of the aorta that forces the heart to pump harder in order to move and circulate her blood.

This could not be happening to us again.

The surgical options the doctor presented were not good. The hypoplastic left heart defect would require either a heart transplant shortly after Neale's birth or a fairly new sequence of surgeries called the Norwood procedure, which would entail three operations before she was eighteen months old. Neale's left heart defect and surgical options were far worse than what we faced with Brock's right heart defect. Jay and I were devastated. We agreed that we didn't know if we had the courage to face one heart surgery, much less three operations. Somehow, we managed to keep going—we didn't have a lot of other options. It was the beginning of Father's Day weekend. Would Jay ever be a father again?

> **"Our hopes were gone. We were devastated."**
>
> ***July 14, 1995***

I quickly scheduled a meeting with the counselor who had helped me process my grief after our loss of Brock. She told me I was making this journey with Neale for a reason and that I must not give up. She said that now more than ever, Neale needed us to be present and positive, and that I needed mentally to separate Brock's life from Neale's life. The counselor suggested to me that I not say or think, "Here we go again." She also advised that I limit my medical research about potential doctors and hospitals for Neale's surgery to a block of time each day, otherwise I would obsess about it twenty-four hours a day. All this was easier said than done. We needed to determine the best option quickly so we could deliver her into the hands of the best doctors to care for her. I left that counselor's office with one goal: I had to be strong for Neale.

Our fetal/pediatric cardiologist suggested that we get a second opinion about Neale's heart. He was a young doctor, and he hoped he was wrong about the diagnosis. We discovered during one of our appointments that this doctor was a believer in the power of prayer. He prayed for us and engaged his friends at his church to intercede for us as well. Our Sunday school class added to the chorus of prayers as we went from one appointment to the next. We shared the details about our appointments and prayer concerns by way of an old-school phone tree that cascaded from voice to voice, to our church friends and to their family and friends. At that time, texting wasn't a thing. I'd dare to say that we had hundreds of people across the country praying for us throughout this journey. We were grateful to have their prayers and support, but we were also burdened by the knowledge of how much we needed them.

My sister Claudia is a pediatrician, and she made some calls to get us a second opinion. She connected us with one of the best fetal cardiologists in the country. He practiced medicine in Boston, so we flew there for an appointment. Our hope was that he would rule out the hypoplastic left heart diagnosis. When we arrived at our appointment, I crawled up onto a table in the dark corner of the patient room. The only light was emanating from the ultrasound equipment. The doctor quietly viewed, measured, and analyzed Neale's heart. Several times, I had to sit up for air and water because I was so anxious during the extensive two-hour ultrasound. A few times, I felt as if I might vomit. When he was done, the doctor left the room to compare her measurements to those of a normal thirty-three-week fetus.

Chapter Two

We reconvened in another room, and the doctor could hardly look at us. Neale's numbers did not look good. They indicated that her left heart would need to grow in order to sustain life after birth. He suggested operating on the aortic coarctation first and then performing the first of the Norwood surgeries shortly after that surgery. Tragically, this second opinion was similar to the first.

We were also scheduled to see a geneticist while we were in Boston. This doctor drew our family tree and discussed possible genetic abnormalities, and she suggested more testing. Jay and I were about to snap. The heart problems were already more than we could handle. Our next appointment was with a maternal-fetal specialist. When we found out that they wanted us to do an additional ultrasound to analyze other parts of Neale, I began to cry uncontrollably. I just couldn't take anymore. We skipped the appointment and got an earlier flight home.

Once home, we continued to search for surgeons and hospitals that could perform infant heart transplants and/or the Norwood procedure. In mid-July, we drove from Greenville, South Carolina, to Egleston Children's Hospital in Atlanta, Georgia. Because they handled both types of operations, we thought they could help us make the decision as to which surgery option was the best. The pediatric cardiologist we met at Egleston performed yet another ultrasound and took measurements of Neale's heart. The news was similar to that which we received in Boston. He said her left ventricle wasn't contracting well, nor was it vigorous.

We asked this cardiologist if this was his child, which surgery would he do—a heart transplant or the Norwood procedure? He stated that he would choose neither option, indicating that he would let her die. His opinion was that it was just not worth it.

What?

Breathless Haste

His words and their implications rattled around in our minds. We were in shock. Here we were with a well-known doctor at a prestigious children's hospital that did both of these types of heart operations, and he was informing us that death was the better option. How much suffering he must have seen in children and parents for him to give us that kind of advice.

Despite the doctor's heart-shattering words, we somehow continued on to our next appointment, which was with one of Egleston's pediatric heart surgeons. He told us that the average wait for an infant heart transplant was one to two months. Ninety percent of heart-transplant children survived the first year and seventy to eighty percent survived after five years. He also shared that two to three daily immunosuppressive medicines are required for transplant recipients, and that long-term use of these could cause cancer or other problems.

He went on to tell us about the Norwood procedure. It was a fairly new surgery, and they didn't have long-term survival rates. After all three surgeries of the Norwood procedure are complete, the child is left with one pumping chamber rather than two chambers. He indicated that a girl who had this procedure done would likely not be able to have children, another arrow in our hearts. I am not sure how Jay was able to drive us home that day.

On Sunday, July 23, 1995, Jay and I walked into our church's chapel for a healing service for Neale. We had never been a part of this type of service before, but a friend had suggested the idea to us. We thought we would just be with ministers for this service, but to our surprise, about thirty people were in attendance, many of whom were members of our Sunday school class. The ministers placed their hands on our shoulders, and the others touched them or us so that each person was touching us through one another, a bit like a human spider web. Each minister prayed aloud for Neale's healing and for our peace to withstand this frightening road ahead. Once they finished, others joined in the chorus of prayers. I felt numb throughout the service, even as tears flowed down my cheeks. Jay said that he felt the power of the focused prayers being offered. Although I believed in my heart that God was definitely present in that room with us, I just couldn't feel Him, nor could I fully comprehend that we were once again in this type of life-and-death situation with a child.

The appointments for ultrasounds continued, along with consultations with neonatologists, maternal-fetal doctors, and cardiologists. We reached out to other families with children with hypoplastic left hearts to discuss the details of their operations, surgeons, and hospitals to help us discern what to do and where to go for surgery. One of the families told me that University of Michigan Hospital had performed one Norwood procedure per week for the past several years. Another family had their son's surgery there as well and had great things to say about the surgeon, staff, and hospital. We began to lean away from the heart transplant option because of the low odds of having access to another child's heart at the time it would be needed and because of the long-term health issues associated with it.

An Ocean

Every year while I was growing up, my family took a week of vacation at Garden City Beach in South Carolina. The beach house sat on the perfect lot. One side of the house faced the ocean, and the other side looked over the marina and inlet. There is something about looking out at any body of water that brings me peace and helps me to realize the vastness of the world in contrast to the smaller day-to-day world I tend

Breathless Haste

to focus on and live in. The long walks on the beach by myself or with family members were always a highlight for my body, lungs, and soul. In the evenings, we would move a couple of long tables together end to end on the screened-in porch, and we would find a variety of chairs so that everyone could have a seat around the table.

One of my sisters loves to cook, and she coordinated the family dinners. We commenced with lighting candles and saying our family blessing, then eating, conversation, and laughter would begin. The ocean sounds and the moon glistening off the water served as the backdrop for our festivities, and as we had many birthdays to celebrate in August, an ice cream cake from the local Baskin-Robbins was always involved. This one week was always the most life-giving, life-resetting time of the year for me. A place for rest and renewal.

So when Brock died, Jay and I headed for the beach, alone this time. It felt like the only place that we could let the tears flow, catch our breath, and regain some sort of footing. The ocean, the sand, the sun, the rhythm of the waves, the sounds and sights of the birds, and the water all brought moments of healing.

I wanted to stay there. I didn't want to go back to the real world, face an empty nursery, or return to work. But somehow, some way, we did make the necessary trip back home. Somehow, we were able to keep putting one foot in front of the other until my pregnancy with Neale.

As Neale's due date approached, my parents reached their fiftieth wedding anniversary, which we had been planning to celebrate for more than a year. Between doctor appointments, I focused on collecting and sorting through fifty years of family pictures so that they could be woven into a video with music to match each decade of photos. I worked on the invitations for the surprise party we were hosting at a beach country club, going through names and addresses of my parents' friends and our extended family. The party would be during the week that the whole family was to be at the beach for our annual gathering.

Jay and I were feeling pulled in two different directions. We wanted to be with the family for the beach week, which we loved, and we wanted to celebrate with my parents, but we were also facing heavy decisions about Neale's surgery. Her due date was only thirty days away. Nervously, we decided to go. We needed an escape, and the distraction would be good.

One morning, I saw Jay in the distance in front of the house sitting on the sand, staring at the ocean for an extended period of time. When he returned, I asked him if he was able to find any answers out there.

He replied, "I didn't find any answers, but I know that the One who created that ocean has the answers."

He reasoned that if God has the power to create that ocean, those tides, and the sky, sun, and earth that surrounded them, then he must also have power over all of creation and human life. I was thankful that Jay thought that God had the answers, and I guess I believed that too. I just wasn't sure that His answers were the answers I desired.

The surprise party blew my parents away. On a beautiful star-filled night, we hosted a seated dinner by the ocean for seventy people. We concluded with the bride and groom cutting a tiered wedding cake for the crowd, and then many of those in attendance stood to give anniversary toasts, including me. I have no idea how I was able to hold a microphone and speak to an audience about my beloved parents, their love, and their faith, while my motherhood was hanging in the balance.

A Billboard

In the fog and confusion of the circumstances we were in, it was too hard for me to hear God's still, small voice, so I had asked God to "paint on a billboard" the hospital we should go to for Neale's surgery. Upon returning from the beach, we were still focused on delivering Neale in Atlanta. It seemed the logical place because of its proximity to our home in Greenville. Michigan was only a passing thought.

On August 7—Brock's birthday, of all days—the Greenville doctors checked Neale's heart again and found that her left heart was growing, but it was still very small. Her heart rate was extremely elevated at 220 to 230 beats/minute. A normal fetal heart rate is typically 130 to 160 beats/minute. The doctors believed that the size discrepancy between the left heart and right heart was causing the problem. They advised that Neale be delivered right away, because they could only control the issue of her high heart rate outside the womb. She was approximately five pounds and twelve ounces, so she was big enough, but they were concerned about her lung development. I asked our two Greenville doctors about their opinion of where the surgery should take place. They both said Michigan. The billboard was beginning to get its first coat of paint.

That afternoon, I was stretched out on the couch at home when the phone rang. This phone call was completely unexpected: it was the pediatric heart surgeon from the University of Michigan Hospital calling me directly. He told me he had looked at Neale's case and agreed that she did have a severe coarctation as well as a small aortic valve that would need to be replaced. He said that her right and left ventricles were the same length, which was an indication that her left heart might not be hypoplastic. He said that he would prefer Neale to be six-and-a-half pounds and thirty-seven weeks before delivery and that she be delivered

Chapter Two

in Michigan. Their hospital system had a private jet that could pick her up for surgery, but a plane ride was not in her best interest, nor was it in mine. He also told me that he had three Norwood procedures on his surgical schedule for that week, giving us more confidence that he was the best surgeon at the best hospital for her case.

The conversation with the surgeon was the final coat of paint we needed on the billboard. We began to pack our bags to fly to Michigan. But to further complicate matters, I began having contractions. My worst nightmare was Neale flying to Michigan for surgery without me. My local doctors decided to put me on a medication called Procardia. Not only did it help to slow my contractions, but it also had a side effect of helping to slow Neale's heart rate.

The doctors checked both Neale's health and mine one more time before our flight. They were ready to use some tough love if necessary, but thankfully they didn't have to; they approved me to fly. On August 11, Jay, my mother, my mother-in-law, and I took the one-and-a-half-hour direct flight to Michigan. Even though we were flying in a plane, it felt more like we were jumping off of a cliff. As we flew, Jay nervously observed me looking at my watch as I had a couple of contractions about five minutes apart during the flight, but I had no other pains after that.

We landed and loaded into a large taxi cab with enough space for four-and-a-half people and our six weeks of luggage. We knew we would be there for delivery, the first Norwood surgery, and a week or two of recovery. We checked into the Med-Inn hotel that was a part of the hospital. My mother and I took a tour of the neonatal intensive care unit (NICU), labor and delivery unit,

"As the nurse showed me labor and delivery, I cried as I told her about Neale and Brock."

August 12, 1995

baby nursery, and cardiac intensive care unit (CICU). Before everything happened, I needed to see where Neale and I would be. Jay was just not up for it, so he stayed back at the hotel. We were both dealing with the enormous stress of the situation the best we could.

The next day, Saturday, August 12, we had an appointment with one of the hospital's pediatric cardiologists. He did yet another ultrasound of Neale's heart and determined that it was still borderline hypoplastic, but because of her position, he couldn't view the aortic coarctation. He indicated that we would need to make some hard decisions when she was born. *We?* The decision would need to be made as to which operation would need to be done first—correcting the aortic coarctation or the hypoplastic left heart. My understanding was if the coarctation was surgically corrected first, the left heart may not be able to withstand the additional blood flow. How would *we* ever be able to decide the order of these operations? We were not capable of making those choices. We were completely dependent on the wisdom of the doctors involved.

The cardiologist suggested that I continue the Procardia medication until I met with the OB/GYN doctors on Monday. If I went into labor over the weekend, they would get the key people to the hospital. But it would be best to deliver during the regular week, if possible, when all of the staff would more readily be available.

We decided to attend the Sunday morning chapel service at the hospital. It was a softly lit small room with stained-glass windows. The chaplain asked if there were any prayer requests. I raised my hand and told of Neale's impending birth and heart surgery, and my mother shared a praise of thanksgiving for our safe arrival.

Chapter Two

The sermon was about worry. The chaplain said, "When we share our sorrows, they are divided, and when our joys are shared, they are multiplied." He continued his talk using the following acrostic for worry:

Wonderful

Opportunity/God's timing

Receive/not just believing, but being in a position to receive His blessings

Riches/God has hundreds of ways to answer our prayers

Yahweh/I am that I am. The greatness of God in comparison to our problems

After the sermon, we sang "God Will Take Care of You," accompanied by a self-playing organ that was in the corner of the chapel. As we walked out, a hospital patient in a wheelchair took my hand and said, "I just feel like that song was meant for your child." God continued to place perfect strangers to encourage us along our path.

On Monday, August 14, Jay and I met with the OB/GYN chief resident of the high-risk obstetrics group at the hospital. He asked why we were there. It took a while to explain the details and get through them without sobbing. He listened with a kind and calm spirit. He then conferred with other doctors and told me to stop the Procardia and let Neale come naturally, whether it be that day, or in a week or two. They then sent us to have a biophysical profile done on Neale to verify that she was practicing breathing, that her heart was beating normally, and that she was showing no signs of stress. All appeared to be going well, so we began our wait, letting nature take its course.

My next pill of Procardia was due at 4:00 p.m., but I wasn't going to take it. At 4:22, my contractions started again, and they were three

Breathless Haste

to five minutes apart. At 5:30, we decided to go out for our last non-hospital meal. As we waited for the taxi, my contractions increased in frequency and grew closer together. Jay, my mother, and mother-in-law kept glancing over at me, and we made the call to cancel our dinner out.

We called the labor and delivery department at about 6:30, and they said I needed to be put on a fetal monitor so they could watch Neale's heart rate and my contractions. Neale's heart rate was back up to more than two hundred beats per minute. We were quickly admitted and set up in a hospital room. At 7:00, the OB/GYN chief resident, the only doctor I knew in all of the state of Michigan, walked into the room. This was such a gift. He knew the heartache and seriousness of our case, and we needed his presence, expertise, and kindness alongside us.

> **"From 3 a.m. to 5:45 a.m., Jay and I dozed on and off as Neale's heart rate continued to beep on the monitor in the room."**
>
> **August 15, 1995**

Because of Neale's high heart rate, he didn't want me to be in labor for too long. At 9:00 p.m., he put me on Pitocin to help induce labor. I hung in there for about six hours, and then I requested an epidural. Somehow, Jay and I dozed on and off as Neale's heart rate continued to beep on the monitor in the room. About 5:45 a.m., I told the doctor that I was having the sensation that I needed to push. He checked me, and Neale's head had crowned. She was ready to come into the world.

Even though I was having a normal delivery, they preferred that high-risk babies be delivered near the NICU staging room, just a few feet from the operating room. Handing Jay blue hospital scrubs to put on, the nurse swiftly began to unhook me from all the equipment. She

Chapter Two

began to push me down the hall in my hospital bed. We were halfway to the operating room before Jay caught up with us.

I was petrified about what was about to happen to Neale. This was the moment I had been dreading—for her, for Jay, and for me. Once the NICU doctors were assembled, I pushed a few times per contraction, and out she popped with a loud cry. It was music to our ears. Earlier, they had indicated that we might not hear her cry because they would be taking her away so quickly. Jay cut the cord, and she was passed into the hands of the neonatologist. The other doctors were waiting for her to come through the doors of the NICU.

They started her on a prostaglandins, a medicine that would enable the ductus in her heart to remain open until surgery. The ductus allows blood to detour away from the lungs before birth. After birth, it closes within days. A child with a hypoplastic left heart cannot survive once the ductus closes, but neither can it remain permanently open. The medicine was intended to provide a temporary fix for a short time frame until the first operation could take place.

A Miracle

Within ten minutes of Neale's delivery, the neonatologist returned and asked Jay if he would like to see her. Of course he did. He came back with the report that she was beautiful, pink, and screaming. Hallelujah!

About three hours after her birth, a pediatric cardiologist walked into our hospital room smiling. He told us that he had done an ultrasound on Neale's heart. He said, "Her left heart is completely normal, and we see no signs of a coarctation. She doesn't have anything that will require surgery."

What did he just say? Was I in a dream?

Breathless Haste

This revelation began slowly to settle into our minds and hearts. The pain and heartache of the nine-month journey began to ease its grip on us. After months of holding our breath, it felt as if we were able to breathe again. Jay and I had a mini revival in the room with my mother and my mother-in-law. There were tears, prayers of thanksgiving, cheers, celebrations, and hugs all around, with one another and with anyone who walked into our hospital room. The nurses and the surgeon joyfully celebrated the good news with us. Most of what they dealt with day to day was so hard for them and the families they worked with. They were excited to be a part of this amazing story.

Our prayers and those that had been lifted on Neale's behalf had been answered in the form of a miracle. Not only had we not personally prayed for that, but never in our wildest dreams had we ever even imagined it. We had prayed ordinary prayers: "Help us get through this appointment. Help her heart to grow. Give wisdom to the cardiologist. Tell us where to have surgery. Keep us safe as we travel." Praying for the extraordinary had never occurred to us—it just seemed too much to ask. Miracles happened in the Bible, but we didn't think about them happening in the here and now. However, I believe our faithful friends and family thought about it and prayed for just that. Without them, I am not sure how this story would have turned out. And in the midst of an ordinary, modern-day hospital operating room, God showed up and showed out for us in an extraordinary healing of our baby girl.

As this revival continued in our hospital room, my father was en route from South Carolina, flying the six hundred miles alone in his little four-seater plane to be with us. Unaware of the news of Neale's delivery or birth, he arrived on the scene in our hospital room. What a

Chapter Two

joy it was to tell him about his granddaughter. He was stunned, and he quickly joined the celebration.

Just when we thought all was well, the cardiologist went on to tell us that Neale's heart rate was still extremely high. For the next couple of days, they shocked her heart and tried different medicines to slow it down. We were getting anxious all over again. They brought in the best doctor in the country for treating electrical heart problems in children. He had written the medical manuals which other doctors learned from, and he worked at the University of Michigan Hospital. He looked at her reports and immediately started her on digoxin and procainamide. One medicine slowed her atria rhythm, and one slowed her ventricle rhythm. Her heart rate responded and slowed to a normal rate. We were so thankful for the wisdom of this doctor God had placed on the scene.

My personal theory about Neale's heart rate is that God made so many last-minute miraculous adjustments to her heart that her heart rate needed some time to adjust as well, not to mention mine.

When our precious baby girl was five days old, they sent us out of the doors of the hospital with her in our arms. We stopped to take family pictures in front of the University Hospital sign. We needed to mark this moment in time in Michigan with a permanent keepsake. We then made our way to the airport with our six weeks of luggage in tow. Much of the clothing remained untouched, as we had only been away from home for eight days. Our Sunday school class of prayer warriors who had walked through this season with us wanted to greet us at the airport in South Carolina. We declined their sweet offer and instead made the quiet journey back home to the fanfare that was happening in our hearts.

Shortly after arriving home, we made an appointment with the cardiologist in Greenville who had seen us throughout the pregnancy.

He had been traveling and had not heard about Neale's arrival. When he saw her name on the schedule, he asked his staff how she could have been born, had surgery, and returned so soon. Once he heard what happened, he asked us to come in for an ultrasound to see for himself. We were weary, but we agreed to one more review.

After completing another ultrasound on Neale, this one outside the womb, he said, "This does not look like the same child. We are witnessing a miracle."

I believe that God sent us to experts all over the country so that there would be no question of a misdiagnosis. Instead, it would be clear that what had happened could only have been a miracle.

The news of the miracle spread quickly. Jay and I, along with Neale's cardiologist, were interviewed by the local television news and the newspaper in Greenville, South Carolina. Apparently, the news traveled from those news channels beyond South Carolina, as we got a call from the *National Enquirer*. At first, we thought it would be great for more people to read about a modern-day miracle, with facts and videos from medical professionals to help prove it. However, we felt like it was such a sacred story that we didn't want it to be tainted, so we said no to that interview.

Neale continued her two medications every six hours until she was nine months old, and then the cardiologist told us to stop the medicine. Her high heart rate did not return. From that point on, her cardiologist invited us to come back for social visits only. Neale has had no additional heart or medical problems. She played softball for ten years, cheered, and did all the normal things girls do. Currently, she is a young adult living in Atlanta, working in advertising and as a Pilates instructor.

Chapter Two

Glory be to God, "who is able to do immeasurably more than all we ask or imagine" (Eph. 3:20).

On the day of Neale's birth, Jay said that our lives would never be the same again. He was so right.

FOR REFLECTION

Take a few minutes to journal in response to these questions:

- ▶ Have you experienced an encounter in nature that made you in awe of the power of God? Where was that for you, and what was it like?
- ▶ When have you prayed for guidance or for God to "paint a billboard" in your life? How did you experience God leading you in this situation?
- ▶ What miracle or extraordinary circumstance have you seen or experienced? How did you feel before and after that experience?

CHAPTER THREE

A Prayer, a Sense of Desperation, and a Cassette Tape (Jay)

> I waited patiently for the LORD; he turned to me and
> heard my cry. He lifted me out of the slimy pit, out of the mud
> and mire; he set my feet on a rock and gave me a firm place to stand.
> He put a new song in my mouth, a hymn of praise to our God.
> Many will see and fear the Lord and put their trust in him.
>
> —PSALM 40:1–3

Hearing the words that Neale's heart was normal and did not require surgery was stunning, a moment in time I vividly remember and yet find hard to fully comprehend, even now. Experiencing the reality of God's healing power in such an intense way still leaves me in awe. The event encompassed in those words changed the trajectory of the rest of our lives. The words that soon flowed from Rebecca were almost as shocking: "We can have another child!"

I could not believe what I was hearing. For Rebecca, the reality that Neale was a healthy baby meant that we could have another healthy child. She immediately saw the miraculous event as opening up a whole world of possibilities. I, on the other hand, felt like someone who had just escaped from a burning building. It was exhilarating, but I had no interest in repeating the experience.

Both of our pregnancies had been extremely traumatic: one ending in heartbreak and the other in wonder. Even in the euphoria of a miracle, fear was still stronger than hope for me. As an only child, I was satisfied to accept this one beautiful example of God's grace and never have to risk the anxiety and potential pain of losing another child. However, from that moment on, Rebecca pondered the dream of another child in her heart and would not allow me to brush it aside.

Just as Rebecca instinctively knew that another child was in our future, I knew that our life would never be the same. I had no idea how it would change, but I knew with certainty that our journey had dramatically shifted in that hospital room. It wasn't possible just to go back to life as usual. Surely God had not done this great thing in a vacuum, for us alone. The words of Psalm 40 resonated in my soul: He had lifted us from the "mud and mire" of tragedy and put a new song in our mouths to sing.

We went back to life as we knew it before, but it was not the same. Rebecca made the decision not to return to her career at IBM. She wanted to fully devote herself to being a mom. I continued in my business with even less passion than before. After my father's death, my primary motivation for spending time with him at work was gone, but I continued to help lead the family business for five more years. In retrospect, that was a mistake. It was not my dream. It had never been my dream. I was just trying to hang on to my dad.

While trying to keep my father's business going, I started another business of my own. I thought that if I could transition from a business in the shrinking textile manufacturing economy into the growing service sector, I would be more energized. In the meantime, we put the family business on the market. When it sold, it was a great relief; however, it also released five years of grief that had been bottled up inside. When my father passed away, I hadn't given myself the space or the permission to grieve. I don't even remember crying. I just stuffed it all inside and tried to be strong for my mom and the business. So, when my dad's business was gone, he was really gone.

One night, I startled awake in the middle of the night, sweating, with my heart practically beating out of my chest. Was I having a heart attack? What was happening? After a few minutes, my heart stopped racing, and I felt normal again. I was able to get back to sleep. That was the first of many anxiety attacks that were to follow in the years ahead. That's what happens when you stuff your emotions, suffer in silence, and try to avoid the God-given tears of grief. You can only outrun the pain of loss for so long before it catches up to you. In addition to the panic attacks, for weeks at a time I felt as if I were in a fog: lacking motivation, just trying to get through the days of building a new business as an entrepreneur. I was in a state of depression.

I eventually spoke with a counselor and tried to process a bit of what had happened, but I really had no idea how to reflect on my story. The counseling was a start, but it would take years to deal with what I was feeling.

A Prayer

After Neale's miraculous birth, I began trying to intentionally live my faith. I was motivated, not by a sense of obligation, but by a growing desire to learn more about Christ and share Him with others. I became

Breathless Haste

a deacon in our church and eventually an elder. One of our pastors, Bob, became a friend and a mentor. He led our men's ministry, and I became very involved and grew in my faith alongside some of my best friends. This was during the rise of the Promise Keepers movement. Like churches all over the nation, we took busloads of men to huge stadium events in several locations. We were inspired by the music, the teaching, and the diversity of these gatherings. It was a spiritual catalyst for many of us, and in a very personal and unexpected way for me.

Our men's group joined hundreds of thousands at the National Mall in Washington, DC, on October 4, 1997, for the Stand in the Gap event. This event brought men together from all over the country to pray for our nation. As the event began, the president of Promise Keepers said to the crowd, "It is possible for you to be at the threshold of a life-changing experience but miss it altogether."

Little did I know that I was at such a threshold. At one point during the event, a speaker asked us to get on our knees—or prostrate, if possible—to put our faces on the ground for prayer. He asked each of us to offer a prayer asking for forgiveness for any way that we had sinned against our wives. I can remember arrogantly thinking that this part did not really apply to me, as I had not been abusive or unfaithful to Rebecca. However, as I lay with my face in the dirt in front of the Smithsonian, the Spirit clearly spoke.

Rebecca had never wavered in her desire for another baby. In the two years since Neale's birth, I had tried to avoid the topic, fearful of having to repeat the pain of our experiences. Rebecca caught me off guard by asking, "Are you praying about it?" The truth was that I was not praying about it, because I was not open to having my mind changed. At that moment on the National Mall, God clearly said, not audibly,

Chapter Three

but in my spirit, "Your wife wants to have another baby, and you will not even pray about it." This moment of prayer that I had thought was not for me turned out to be specifically for me. I could clearly see that my unwillingness to be open to this possibility was harming Rebecca, and it was harming my relationship with God. It was a humbling and convicting experience.

On the bus ride back to South Carolina, I shared the experience with our group. Then, when I returned home, I shared it with Rebecca. I committed myself to praying about having another child. In doing so, I stepped through a threshold of openness to the will of God, even if it meant facing my fears.

About six months later, Rebecca was expecting our third child. That experience provided a lesson that I needed to learn and have had to relearn time and again. We find God in the ordinary, and we experience his power when we are open to hearing Him and responding to His voice. The willingness to be open to whatever He says is one of the critical elements of experiencing Him in our lives.

This third pregnancy was far different from the others. Because of our experiences with Brock and Neale, we had to undergo a level 2 ultrasound once again. There was tremendous anxiety during that process. I remember sitting in yet another dark ultrasound room with Rebecca, just waiting for another dreaded diagnosis. The technician asked Rebecca if she wanted to know the gender. She said yes, and we were told that we were expecting a baby boy. Rebecca said that at that moment she knew in her spirit everything would be fine. That news of having another son brought tears to my eyes; it was a dream I had let go of, honestly believing it would never happen. The cardiologist arrived, performed the detailed ultrasound, and soon confirmed Rebecca's sense that all was well. It was such a relief to hear that our son was healthy.

The rest of the pregnancy went smoothly. In fact, on the day of the delivery, our son came so quickly that our doctor did not even have time to get to the hospital. After years of us researching the best physicians to care for our children, William Edward was delivered by a hospital resident.

When William was born, the hospital staff simply handed him to us and left the room. For a couple used to deliveries surrounded by teams of medical professionals and life-and-death decisions, this moment was at once strange and glorious. As I held my son, I finally knew why people enjoyed having babies. The births of our children had revealed the grace of God through the tragic, the miraculous, and now the ordinary.

Years later, William tagged along with me when I attended a prayer conference in Washington, DC. While there, we visited the monuments that are there to remind us of some of our most significant leaders and moments in history. I took along with me a picture of the 1997 Promise Keepers event, which displayed the National Mall filled with men. I showed William the place where I opened myself up to God and heard His voice. That is a spiritual monument for our family. It marks a moment of experiencing God's presence that blessed us with a son and expanded our faith for the journey ahead.

A Sense of Desperation

From all outward appearances, our life was awesome. We loved one another, had two wonderful children, and lived in our dream house. All was well, except for the way I spent most of my days. Even though I owned my own business, I felt completely unfulfilled and was essentially

Chapter Three

going through the motions. After selling the family business, I continued to operate my new business and eventually developed a real-estate project as well. I liked being an entrepreneur and starting new things.

However, ultimately, it was never more than a way to pay the bills. It did not give me joy, nor did it feed my soul. I also spent a good deal of time helping Rebecca's father with his farm. I loved the cattle and being outdoors, and I even wondered if we should eventually move there and carry on that family tradition. During those years, my business became more difficult. As the frustrations began to mount, so did my stress level. In short, I was miserable.

Like many men in their thirties, I had a receding hairline. However, I also noticed that I had places where my hair was disappearing, leaving smooth bald spots. My barber told me that he knew other people with the same condition and that he had heard it might be related to stress. Well, that made sense! I soon learned that what I had was called alopecia areata. Basically, your immune system attacks your hair follicles. In many cases, it stops, and your hair grows back, but for others, like me, it lingers, sometimes forever. I tried a lot of different remedies, but nothing was effective. I finally decided to stop fighting it and just shave my head. Neale loved the movie *Annie*, and I told her I was going to look like Daddy Warbucks. It was actually a liberating decision. At the time, I didn't know just how many bald jokes were in my future. It was and is still painful; however, it increased my ability to feel for people who look different and feel out of place. It made me look like a totally different person, and in some ways, it was a metaphor for the other changes that were coming.

Breathless Haste

I began to read books such as *Halftime: Moving from Success to Significance* by Bob Buford[1] and *If You Want to Walk on Water, You've to Get Out of the Boat* by John Ortberg.[2] I resonated with the words of these authors and the idea of moving from "success to significance." I had a sense that I was wasting my life. The years were slipping by, and I was living in a small story. I felt stuck. I wanted my life to change, and I wanted to play a role in serving and impacting the lives of others—but how would that happen? How could I extricate myself from this business? And if that happened, what would I even do? I had many more questions than answers.

We most clearly hear God's voice when we are willing to follow wherever He leads, when we are most open, and when we are desperate. I had a growing sense of desperation. One morning, I was already at my business at 6:00 a.m., dealing with a crisis. In a moment of despair, I went into my office and left a message for a business broker, asking him to find someone to buy my business. As I hung up, I prayed, "God, if You will get me out of this business, I will do whatever You want, but I can't do this anymore." The word *whatever* must be part of God's love language, because within a matter of weeks, the broker had found a buyer.

The deal was not perfect from a financial standpoint, but from the perspective of answered prayer, it seemed divine. I decided to take the opportunity to close that chapter of my life and step into the unknown.

After we closed, Rebecca said, "I guess this means you're really going to get out of the boat."

---

1 Bob Buford, *Halftime: Moving from Success to Significance* (Grand Rapids, MI: Zondervan, 2011).
2 John Ortberg, *If You Want to Walk on Water, You've Got to Get Out of the Boat* (Grand Rapids, MI: Zondervan, 2014).

I replied, "No, this means I'm already out of the boat."

Selling your business and not having to go to work sounds glamorous. However, that was not really the case for me. I was mid-career, with a young family, a mortgage, a vague sense of calling to "ministry," and no clue what that was going to look like. I had leaped into a stream with a strong current, but I didn't know where it was going. Regardless of not knowing where the water was taking me, it felt good finally to be on the move after several years of feeling stuck.

A Cassette Tape

I did not see myself as a pastor. That seemed like a bizarre idea, and even all these years later, it sometimes still does. I envisioned myself working for a nonprofit organization, not in a button-down shirt and a robe. Honestly, I just wanted to make a difference with my life. As I began to wonder about where God was leading, I was approached with an opportunity from our church. My mentor was retiring, and the executive pastor asked me whether I would be willing to fill his role while they searched for a permanent replacement. It's interesting how God's timing works through our relationships. Bob had encouraged me in ministry when I was a young leader, and now his transition was opening the door for my next step. Rebecca and I talked and prayed about it, but honestly, it was an easy decision. It was an opportunity for what Bob Buford, in his book *Halftime*, describes as a "low-cost probe."[3] There was not much risk. I could transition to ministry with the same church, same house, and same friends. Being out of the boat was not as hard as I had imagined! In fact, I loved it. For the first time in years, I looked forward to getting to work. I had the opportunity to focus on

---

3 Buford, *Halftime,* 104.

what I was passionate about and even lead people to Christ. Finally, my vocation seemed to fit.

In October, a few months into the role, I had the opportunity to attend an evangelism conference at a megachurch near Chicago, with a friend. I was taken aback by the size, the music, and the innovation there, which was in sharp contrast to my more traditional church experience. While there, I learned that they had initiated a church leadership internship program that included seminary, ministry experience, and spiritual formation. I snuck away to a presentation about this program. It was an interesting concept, but it seemed like such a crazy idea that I didn't even tell the friend I was with about it.

As the months passed, the idea of being called as a pastor began to rapidly crystallize for me. In late October 2002, a couple of weeks after returning from Chicago, I had to go to my former business to talk over an issue with the new owners. On the way, I was listening to a sermon on a cassette tape from this megachurch in my car. As I sat in the parking lot, John Ortberg described the parable of the hidden treasure: The kingdom of heaven is like treasure hidden in a field. When a man found it, he hid it again, and then in his joy went and sold all he had and bought that field. (Matt. 13:44)

Ortberg said, "This is the chance of a lifetime—the surrender of a lesser, dying futile self for a greater eternal one, the person God planned for you to be."

"I think I need to do ministry but how and where?"

January 18, 2003

At that moment, I felt God's presence, certain that those words I heard while sitting in a dark parking lot were meant just for me. In joy, I was leaving my old life behind for something of much greater value, following His calling on my life, and really becoming the man I was created to be. I now knew this was my path, but I still had no idea where it would lead. I was in an interim position, and because I had not been to seminary, remaining in that role at First Presbyterian was not an option.

That became even clearer on January 5, 2003. That morning I served Communion to Neale for the first time, which was a special experience, as her story was such a crucial part of God's leading in my life. After that service, the executive pastor shared that the search committee had found a candidate for my role, and it was on the fast track. I appreciated the heads-up but that news made me sad. I had enjoyed those months of church work. It seemed to fit me like a glove, and it was comfortable. In retrospect, it was too comfortable. I went home and told Rebecca that I sensed that the easy part of this journey was coming to an end.

FOR REFLECTION

Take a few minutes to journal in response to these questions:

- ▶ Have you ever felt stuck in your career or stage of life? How did you respond?
- ▶ When have you experienced a season of discontent that convinced you that you needed to make a change? What was the catalyst for change in your life?
- ▶ Are you really open to whatever God might say to you about your life or career? Why or why not?
- ▶ Can you think of a time when you felt prompted by God? What words have you heard in a song, sermon, or Scripture that moved you?

CHAPTER FOUR

A Clock, a Song, and a Mortgage (Rebecca)

> *"For I know the plans I have for you," declares the LORD, "plans to prosper you and not to harm you, plans to give you hope and a future. Then you will call on me and come and pray to me, and I will listen to you. You will seek me and find me when you seek me with all your heart. I will be found by you," declares the LORD, "and will bring you back from captivity. I will gather you from all the nations and places where I have banished you," declares the Lord, "and will bring you back to the place from which I carried you into exile."*
>
> —JEREMIAH 29:11–14

It was immediately apparent that what Jay had said about our lives never being the same again after Neale's miracle was true. Our faith had grown exponentially that day, so we became increasingly active in our church. I had come a long way: from not attending church at all to attending church all the time. My life and my faith were becoming much more interwoven. As Jay was settling into his temporary role as a pastor, I also was pouring myself out at church as a way to thank God for our miracle with my whole being. I was in the choir, led a Moms in Touch prayer group, and participated in many Bible studies. For our beloved Sunday school class, I coordinated the welcoming of visitors, and I created care groups as the class continued to grow.

When Jay returned home from Chicago, he told me all about the conference and the church leadership internship. The internship details lodged in my heart, but because it was so far from where we lived, I did not see it as a possibility for us. It was just too far away from the life we lived, too far from where our history was, and too far from our deep Southern roots.

In November 2002, because of all my frenetic church activity, along with caring for two young children, I felt as if I were having a minor nervous breakdown. I was overwhelmed. A question spontaneously came to my mind during that time: Of all these types of activities, which would I continue to do if we moved? It was an odd thought, because it occurred long before we were even considering a move. I think God was giving me advance notice as a way to prepare me. I decided to let go of choir, my prayer group, and my Sunday school leadership duties. The process of disconnecting from things I was passionate about felt very odd, because I didn't understand the why behind it. However, I continued to move forward, trusting God.

A Clock

A couple of months later, Jay knew his interim role as pastor was sadly drawing to a close. It was the first job in his life he had loved and the first to which he had felt called. Without asking or telling me, he decided to call the church to learn more about the internship. (I think he was pretty sure I would stop him in his tracks.) They told him that

Chapter Four

he was very late in the process but that we should come to Chicago in a couple of weeks for the internship training weekend. Jay told me about this call and their response. I was taken aback and reacted with a loud, "No! You

> **"Jay calls and asks if we could go to Chicago . . . I took a shower and boo-hooed. Is he serious? I've never lived outside SC. My parents would die."**
>
> **January 6, 2003**

check out all the other seminaries and all the other options. If after a few months, you still are interested, I will go with you then." I wanted to scream. My heart's desire was to find a path that would allow us to stay right where we were—in our forever home, near our forever friends and family.

Shortly after that intense discussion, Jay went away for his annual duck hunting trip with his friends and our beloved chocolate Labrador, Genny. The first night he was away, I woke up and looked over at the old brown plastic clock next to my bed. The bright red digits read 4:30. It was very dark outside. The children were still young, and they were typically the only reasons I would wake up in the middle of the night. But they were both asleep. This was highly unusual for me, but I rolled over and went back to sleep.

The second night of his absence, I woke again. I glanced at the clock—the big red numbers showed 4:30 again, not 4:25 or 4:32. Once more, I rolled over and returned to sleep. The third night, another awakening—it was 4:30 a.m. I finally tossed back the covers and very irreverently said, "Okay, God. What is it?"

I got up and plopped into the red chaise lounge chair right next to my bed, the place where I most often read and prayed. The book *The*

Power of a Praying Wife by Stormie Omartian[4] was lying face down on my chair, open to chapter 9. I had been praying the prayers outlined on the pages almost daily, but I hadn't been reading the actual text of the chapters. Not knowing what else to do, I began to read the contents of chapter 9, titled "His Purpose": "Everyone has a purpose. It's the reason we exist. . . . When [your husband] discovers that purpose, and is doing what he was created to do, becoming what he was created to be, he will find fulfillment. This can only contribute to *your* happiness as well."[5] The tears began to flow as I turned each page. It was as if God were writing on the pages of this book with a black marker, "Go to Chicago!"

Surely God wasn't asking me to leave everything I had ever known. My quiet tears turned into sobbing.

As I reflect on this encounter, I am struck by the similarities between it and Jay's experience at Promise Keepers, when God spoke to him about me and my desire for another baby. In this instance, it was God speaking to me about Jay and his purpose. Jay and I both heard from God in different ways in these situations. Because each of us was open to God's guidance and wanted His best for the other, it strengthened our marriage. Wanting God's best for your spouse is a gift to them.

I called my dear friend Melody a few hours after my early morning awakening. We met for a walk. I shared with her what had happened, and the tears continued to flow as we followed the long path in the park. She told me that Jay and I had to go to investigate the internship, and she offered to watch our children. I knew in my head that she was right, but my heart was aching, and I could not stop thinking about the implications of this situation. Jay called later that day, and I explained

---

4 Stormie Omartian, *The Power of a Praying Wife* (Eugene, OR: Harvest House, 2014).
5 Omartian, *Power of a Praying Wife,* 93–95.

the events of the early morning and what I thought God was telling me. He was blown away.

Jay never pushed this internship on me. He knew that we were in this together, so he patiently waited for God to bring us together on any decision for our future. I think if I had been in his position, I would have prodded, pushing the idea harder and arguing with him. Instead, he let God do the work in me. In the long run, that is the best approach, but it requires patience in the waiting.

My mind began constantly to churn on just the possibility of moving. I worried about schools, leasing our house, and packing. I am a planner and organizer, so that is where my thoughts tend to go. I was sad and anxious about all of it. One morning before Bible study, I went to church early and found my way to the chapel to catch up on my *Breaking Free* study homework.[6] I couldn't get the lights on in the chapel, so I just sat down on one of the church pews. The morning sunlight poured through the stained-glass window, shining on the spot right where I was sitting. I began to read, and this is what Beth Moore said in the pages of her study: "Have you sometimes experienced defeat because you refused to calm yourself in the presence of God and trust Him? . . . Once we've obeyed God, we can do nothing more. We then wait on Him to bring the victory, knowing the consequences of our obedience are His problem and not ours."[7] As the potential challenges of moving to Chicago spun around in my head, I had to remember that those were God's problems, not mine.

The pastoral candidate quickly accepted the full-time position at First Presbyterian, so Jay's days of working in his interim role were

---

6 Beth Moore, *Breaking Free: Making Liberty in Christ a Reality in Life* (Nashville, TN: Lifeway, 1999).
7 Moore, *Breaking Free*, 144.

numbered. It felt as if we had buckled in for a roller-coaster ride that had just left the platform. Things were accelerating quickly.

We decided to take a trip to see my parents, who were in their eighties. We felt it was time to start the conversation with them about this potential internship, even though it seemed premature. We told my father that a new minister was being hired, and my father's initial response was to ask Jay to come help him farm. He had always longed to see us move to Florence, South Carolina, to live in the old homeplace and continue the farm that had been in our family for three generations. As we continued the discussion of the details of what was happening in our hearts and souls, I am sure this news of a potential job in Chicago was extremely hard for my father to hear. There was no one else in our family who wanted the opportunity to farm. Who would live in the home? How would the farm go on? But before the conversation finished, my father said to us, "One generation can't tell the next generation what to do."

He was willing to let us go, even though it must have been so painful for him. We were not only saying no to him and no to the farm, but also limiting the frequency of family visits. The distance between him and his daughter, son-in-law, and grandchildren would be a daunting fourteen-hour drive instead of three.

At about the same time, my mother-in-law, Sara, who was in her sixties, found out that she had a blood cancer called multiple myeloma. Jay is an only child, so this news was even more difficult in light of what we were considering. Fortunately, our minds were eased because Sara had remarried and had a wonderful husband, Fred, who took care of her every need. But we still knew that it would be best for us to be nearby.

Chapter Four

We decided not to share with them all the details of this opportunity until we were more sure about the internship.

Our desire to honor and care for our parents seemed in complete opposition to what we thought we were being led to do. If we were in Chicago, how could we care well for aging or ill parents in South Carolina?

A week or so later, we took a 5:50 a.m. flight to attend the internship retreat. It was the only flight we could afford with our frequent flier points. Oddly enough, it was snowing that morning in South Carolina, so the plane had to be de-iced, but we finally made it to Chicago by way of a flight change in Dallas. Later, we found out that the 11:00 a.m. direct flight we had wanted to take had been canceled due to the snow and the shutdown of the interstate. We would have missed much of the internship gathering had we been on that flight. God continued to show up in every little detail.

We arrived in Chicago to a sub-zero windchill, picked up the rental car, and made our way to the church. The intensity of the cold weather took our breath away. The internship gathering included about twenty people who were applying for the program that was to begin a few months later. Many of these intern applicants had been in the process for at least a year.

On Saturday night, we attended the church service, which just *happened* to be Vision Night, an annual event attended by thousands of people. My traditional church experience was being stretched in every way—through words, sights, and sounds. I had never been a part of a service like that before. The service was held in an auditorium with theater style seating for 4,500 people. It had a massive center stage with digital screens on either side and large windows overlooking a lake to the right and to the left—no pews, no stained-glass, no hymnals, no organ, no choir anywhere in sight. The voices and sounds of the incredible musicians and full band joined by a room full of people standing and singing passionately gave me goosebumps. The senior pastor's words and vision casting about the gospel and the future of the church were powerful and moving. My soul was filled and overwhelmed at the same time. He explained that the church hosted about nineteen thousand people each weekend during four services, and that about ten thousand churches were connected with the church association. This was a far cry from my church experience with hundreds of people attending a service week to week. I found it completely mind-boggling.

The pastor spoke of the ten values of the church, which included anointed biblical teaching, how lost people matter to God, and that the church is led by those with leadership skills. The final value was full devotion to Christ—taking the hand of Christ and leaving your agenda behind. Gulp. I like having my own agenda.

A Song

The weekend continued with us learning more about the details of the internship with the other prospective interns and their spouses in a small, dark conference room. In addition to the presentations, we had times of reflection. The internship director prayed using the exact same words— "created to be and created to do"—that I had read at 4:30 a.m. in *The Power of a Praying Wife* a few weeks earlier. We then sat quietly to process and pray, as a song titled "Open Up" by Greg and Corinne Ferguson[8] played in the background. Here are some of the words that hung in the air:

---

8 Greg and Corinne Ferguson, "Open Up" (Willow Creek Association, 2002).

Chapter Four

If I never take a chance and pray
How'm I gonna know if You're gonna answer
Is there somethin' that You wanna say
Do You wanna keep me from some disaster

I wanna make a wager of faith
I wanna put my trust on the line
So I'm gonna open the door
And pour my heart out to You

Lord if I open up
And tell you everything that's on my mind
How can I know for sure
That You're gonna give me a reply

Lord if I let it fly
And open up the lines of communication
Will there be miracles
Am I gonna find You've been here all the time
All the time

I know I'm not gonna say it right
I'm not gonna think about the punctuation
Nothin's gonna be a big surprise
You already know about my situation

I wanna make a wager of faith
I wanna put my pride on the line
I'm gonna let my knees hit the floor
And pour my heart out to You.

Breathless Haste

As the song played, I pulled my chair back from the table, leaned forward, put my arms on my legs, and lowered my head until it hung between my knees. I remember my tears dripping directly onto the carpet below. I was swept away in a moment of trying to surrender fully to God. The words of the song felt as if they were written specifically for me at this exact point in time, at this crossroads in my life. I was completely undone.

A woman on the church staff noticed that I was struggling. At the next break, she kindly asked how she might be able to help. I launched into several of the questions that were swirling around in my head, one of which was where we would live. She offered to drive us around the area later that day. One of the neighborhoods we toured was Algonquin Lakes, about twenty minutes from the church. It was a new neighborhood with a new elementary school. I vividly remember taking a mental snapshot of the elementary school and the street it was on, all covered in snow. It became seared in my memory.

Jay and I returned to the hotel and discussed the events of the day. I asked Jay, "If God had asked us before Neale's birth if we would move to Chicago as a trade for the miracle of her life, would we have taken the offer?" We both agreed without a doubt that we would. So why now, after the miracle, would we not take it?

We still had so many mixed emotions, but we both felt sure that we were to continue to pursue this option, all the while praying that God would close the door. At the end of the weekend, we returned home. Jay wanted to explore other opportunities, so he visited Gordon-Conwell Seminary in Charlotte, North Carolina, to discuss their seminary options. While there, Jay talked with the Admissions Advisor, who asked what other options he was considering. Jay mentioned the internship, and the advisor said that he had attended the church where the internship was being offered. He went on and on, raving about the church there. He barely talked at all about the seminary he was representing. Jay walked away from the meeting shaking his head and laughing.

A few days later, Jay was going through the friendship/visitor pad papers at First Presbyterian so he could contact any new people who had visited for the first time. He came across one entry that caught his attention, the name of a student from a local university in South Carolina with a note that mentioned that he was a member of the church we'd visited in Chicago. All of these events individually would not have been worthy of mention, but lined up collectively, it seemed that God was using each one to get our attention.

Jay talked to another pastor on staff at First Presbyterian about the internship. Jay thought he wouldn't think highly of it since he had a traditional perspective on theology and the church. Instead, this pastor said this opportunity, combined with a degree from seminary, would be like getting a Harvard MBA. Jay also spoke at length with his mentor. Once this mentor heard the details, he offered to support us financially.

The promptings, signs, and conversations continued to point us in the direction of Chicago and gave us the courage to move forward.

A week after we returned from Chicago, Jay and the internship director spoke over the phone and mutually discerned that Jay needed to take the next step. So Jay filled out the internship application and sent it in. He flew back to Chicago for a grueling set of nine interviews scheduled over several days. Apparently, this internship was very serious business. We found out that they limited the program to approximately ten interns per year. Jay met with a wide array of ministry leaders, but he had the best connection and interview with those leading the evangelism ministry. They told him they had been praying for someone to lead their groups of new believers.

Between interviews, Jay left the church to catch his breath and to look at rental house options for our family. Most of what he looked at was expensive, old, and dirty. He knew I would not be pleased. One option that he discovered was in the new neighborhood we had seen just a couple of weeks earlier. The elementary school could be seen from the front door. It was almost the exact location where I had taken the mental snapshot in that neighborhood. It had recently been leased, but the realtor said she thought the lease might fall through, so Jay was able to see it. It was an almost new, very clean house with three bedrooms, and it would be available on May 1. The internship was to begin in June. It was so much better than anything else on the market that Jay offered her earnest money just to have the option. Things seemed to be getting very serious, very quickly.

Jay's last conversation regarding the opportunity was with the internship director. She told him that it was a definite yes and a done deal. She said that they had never had anyone come in this late in the internship process and get accepted. God was clearing the way for us.

We began the hard conversations with friends and family about what we felt God was calling us to do. Some cheered us on, and I'm sure some thought we were crazy. During the

> **"William told his best friend that we were moving 'because God told us to.'"**
>
> **February 28, 2003**

next conversation with my father—a devoted Christian, mind you—he told me he would pay us to stay and continue the family farm. He was still trying to hang on to us. I don't think he or others understood at the time how deeply we felt called to this opportunity. I explained to my father that this calling had nothing to do with money. As a matter of fact, this was an unpaid three-year internship. Most interns raised full support to be able to participate. We raised a little money, but we planned to live on a tight budget and on the business income we had.

Everywhere we turned, "I know the plans I have for you" (from Jeremiah 29:11–14) showed up in our lives. It showed up in our email inboxes, in notes from friends, and even in a sermon at my parents' church.

> *"Mama said, 'When you believe in God's word and I do. And you believe that God speaks to you and I do. I am still not crazy about this, but I know it's what you are supposed to do.'"*
> **Late March 2003**

After hearing it, my mother said that if I had heard that sermon, I would be going to Chicago tomorrow. I was so thankful that God was speaking to her about us. What a gift!

Jay wrote my father a long, heartfelt letter about how hard it was to leave him, the beloved farm, and the cows. Jay had spent many days on the farm after Brock's death, building fences and tending to the cattle. It was a time of healing for him. At the bottom of the letter, he wrote the verses from Jeremiah and underlined part of verse 14, "bring you home again to your own land" (NLT). Our hope was that these words were an assurance that we would return one day. We honestly thought we would return to First Presbyterian and to our beloved Greenville home, which made the idea of leaving a bit easier. However, one of my Sunday school friends told me that she didn't think God led in a circle. Her words have stuck with me throughout the years.

A Mortgage

During the transition, one of Jay's dearest high school friends called to hear the details of this opportunity. We weren't sure where he stood with his faith, but he asked Jay how he could be praying for us. Jay told him that he was most concerned about the financial strain. We were going to have to continue to pay our mortgage until our Greenville house was either leased or sold, and in Chicago we would also have to pay rent that was more than what we paid on our home mortgage. This friend responded to our predicament by saying, "I'll pay your mortgage until you sell or rent your home."

When Jay hung up the phone, he shared this astonishing news with me. We were completely blown away. It was another sign that God was confirming this move for us in a tangible way.

In addition to being open to God's plan for Jay's work, we had to be open to being humble and accepting the generosity that people offered to us. We had never been in this position before. It was awkward, humbling, and encouraging all at the same time. Our Sunday school class friends continued to love and pray for us as we began to make the transition. They hosted a large going-away party for us, and they gave us a most beautiful gift of a large framed print of Jeremiah 29:11. That gift hangs in our house today to remind us of our community of faith.

We signed a lease on the house in Algonquin Lakes, which I had only seen in pictures. It took quite a leap of faith for me to rent a house sight unseen! I obtained the floor plans so I could begin to plan and organize. I picked out furniture from our house that would fit in this small home and decided what would go in storage. I priced moving boxes and began to feel upset over how much everything was going to cost. The financial stress was already getting to me. But shortly after this, I learned that the pastor who was taking Jay's job was moving into his house and that we could have all their boxes for free. Again, God continued to show up, even in the smallest of details.

Chapter Four

Jay went to Chicago ahead of me to get us moved into the house. Several of Jay's friends wanted to see the Chicago area, so they accompanied him in the moving process. They provided the free labor to help get us settled in. One of those dear friends even spent hours assembling a kitchen table and cabinet for us, and another bought a large supply of toilet paper to get us started. Support from friends for this crazy leap of faith came in a variety of sincere, generous, and funny ways.

When Jay returned from Chicago, we packed up our gray Honda minivan with a four-year-old, a seven-year-old, our beloved Labrador, and our personal belongings. Our heads and hearts were full of forty years' worth of memories of life in South Carolina. We left our families, our friends, our church, our home, and everything we had ever known. We felt as if we were jumping off a cliff, again.

FOR REFLECTION

Take a few minutes to journal in response to these questions:

▶ What have you been nudged to do multiple times? Did you follow through? Why, or why not?

▶ Whose voices do you consult for guidance when making big decisions? Have you ever sensed God's leading through the words of a trusted family member or friend?

▶ Has someone blown you away with their generosity? If so, what was it? Do you recognize it as a gift from God?

CHAPTER FIVE

Jenga, a Tree, and a Mentor (Jay)

> *The Lord is my shepherd; I shall not want.*
> *He makes me lie down in green pastures.*
> *He leads me beside still waters.*
> *He restores my soul.*
>
> —Psalm 23:1–3, ESV

We have a picture of our home in South Carolina with both "for sale" and "for lease" signs in the front yard. Looming in the background is an eighteen-wheeler truck emblazoned with the words, "Chicagoland Moving and Storage." That photo summed up our transition perfectly. It is one thing to believe that you have heard God's voice. It is another to actually follow through on it. On the one hand, it was exhilarating to be throwing caution to the wind and following God on a midlife adventure. On the other hand, it was gut-wrenching to be walking away from our home, our family, and the friends whom we had been sure we would do life with forever. These were the people who shared in our best and worst of times. This was the house where we brought our children home after they were born and where we had lunch after Brock's funeral. We were leaving behind so many memories. As Rebecca said, "Leaving this house is killing me."

We had two signs in our yard, but we clearly had one preference. As we drove away on May 19, 2003, our thought was that we would be gone for three years and then come back. That would allow me time to complete seminary, gain valuable ministry experience, and lastly—or so I thought—become spiritually formed. Whatever that meant.

We moved into our home in Chicago and tried to acclimate to our new surroundings before I left for a two-week seminary intensive. During my first days at the church, we were in the office to sign some paperwork. The church CFO saw us and introduced himself. He asked the kids how they liked being here. Five-year-old William, really leaning into his new life as a pastor's kid, said, "I 'yike' it all except for the church part."

During the first few weeks, everyone in the internship program had a chance to go to the senior pastor's vacation home in Michigan and spend the afternoon listening to him talk about leadership. He was the founder of the church and the author of several ministry leadership books. I was excited about the opportunity to meet him and learn from his experience. He shared some leadership tips that I still remember all these years later. However, the thing that I remember the most is the ride back to Chicago. I was shocked by some of the comments of those who had been in the internship program for a couple of years. They were angry with the senior pastor and very cynical about the church and its leadership. One of the interns even challenged me in a conversation, because he learned that I came from a Presbyterian background. He wanted to have a theological debate before I had even had my first

Chapter Five

day in seminary. It was all very confusing. It would take time before I understood the source of their frustration.

We had assumed we could easily find a long-term renter for our home in Greenville. That happened quite a lot in our area because it was the headquarters for a number of international corporations. However, as the weeks went by, we had only one prospect, and they needed to sell their house before they could lease ours. The tension mounted. In early July, we received a full-price offer to buy our house. It was a huge blessing, except for the fact that in our hearts we really did not want to sell it. However, we couldn't ask my friend to continue to help with our mortgage while we held out for a renter. I wrote in my journal, "This is part of the journey of letting go of one more thing—the most visible sign of our life that was." I resonated with the words of Robert Frost in his poem "The Road Not Taken." I could see this moment in my life in his words, "Two roads diverged in a yellow wood / and sorry that I could not travel both." I was feeling torn by the desire to hold on to our old life and begin a new one. I wanted to return to the comfort of this house and this community, but "Yet knowing how way leads on to way, / I doubted if I should ever come back."⁹

Jenga

Letting go of that house was part of a great deal of deconstruction in many areas of our lives. Over the next couple of years, many things that I believed and had experienced would be pulled apart. Those years in Chicago forced me to grapple with what I believed about my family, the church, and even Jesus. During my first year of seminary, an old friend asked if I had gotten all of my questions answered. I responded

---

9 Robert Frost, "The Road Not Taken," *Mountain Interval* (New York, Henry Holt: 1915), 9.

that I now just had more complicated questions. It had been a long time since I had been in school, so reading a massive book in my first class on hermeneutics made me wonder if this was all a mistake. I soon gained confidence that I could do the work, but I also began to realize that it was all much more complicated than I had imagined.

Many people enter seminary believing that they are there simply to learn the right information to support their current beliefs. However, what happens more often is a realization that some of our beliefs won't hold up to rigorous thought or study. There is more nuance and mystery in Scripture than we can imagine. This type of deconstruction is unsettling and even causes some people to question their faith. Like a game of Jenga, once you take out a few pieces of wood, the whole thing can crumble, and it can be difficult to put back together. I had gotten a glimpse of that in the car ride back from the meeting with the senior pastor. Over time, deconstruction eventually leads some people closer to God and their community, while others become cynical and toxic. As time went by, I came to the conclusion that the purpose of seminary is not to stuff God into a preconceived, man-made box, but to expand our knowledge of the things of God, even if they contradict our prior beliefs. In this way, we will be better equipped to communicate the hope of Christ to the world.

Thankfully, I never really wavered in the core of my faith. In God's grace, I acquired stronger materials for rebuilding the areas that were weakened. In fact, I enjoyed the learning. Some classes and professors were better than others, but in the end, as with all academic pursuits, I got out of it what I put into it. Attending seminary while serving at this church was a bit odd in itself. I had come from a Presbyterian culture that viewed seminary education as necessary just to operate the copier,

Chapter Five

and now I was serving at a church that saw it as practically a waste of time. They had many seminary-trained pastors, but probably the majority—including the senior pastor—were not. After all, there were souls to save. Why waste time sitting in a classroom discussing it?

The internship included a three-year master's degree distance program with a focus on Christian leadership through Bethel Seminary in St. Paul, Minnesota. However, I knew that in a more traditional environment, the master of divinity (MDiv) was the gold standard. I did some research and found that it was possible to make the switch to the MDiv degree. But that would require an additional year of school and a heavier academic load. Each morning, I was up early spending a couple of hours on school before going to work. It took a tremendous amount of self-discipline to do well in this type of distance-learning format. I can vividly remember the feeling in the pit of my stomach when each semester I would get the syllabus for two classes. How could I complete all the assignments, read the books, and write the papers while working and trying to be a husband and father? I learned that the only way to make it work was to sit down and make appointments on my calendar to complete every assignment early in the mornings. Once I did that, I could see a path through the semester.

Why would I want to spend four years doing this seminary work, along with seventeen weeks of intensives in St. Paul, for a church environment that did not value it? At the same time, I sensed that this choice would provide the most options for me wherever God might lead. At that point, going forward, I saw myself in a nondenominational church environment. However, I continued to feel a deep connection to where I had been. My closest friend in the program, Barry (also from a more traditional church background), had the same inclination. So, in the midst of our first grueling year of seminary, we made the decision to add another.

A Tree

I remember well that first seminary intensive during the winter in Minnesota. Rebecca remembers it well too, as a large storm hit while I was away, and she was left shoveling snow in the driveway alone. Under her breath, she muttered to the world, "Don't people know that you don't have to live like this?" Meanwhile, I was trying to dig my way through a systematic theology class. I was also feeling overwhelmed, but my concern was with theological concepts. I felt that there was no way I could take it all in and reconcile it in my mind. During a break, I stood looking out a window as huge flakes of snow fell toward the ground. I vividly remember watching a tree gradually being covered in snow. There was a crook in the tree where the snow was collecting. While most fell to the ground, some were caught by the shape of the tree. As I watched the snow accumulating in the crook of the tree, God used that image as a moment of assurance. I felt as if I were standing in a blizzard of theological concepts, but that all I needed would stick and provide nourishment. I could rest in that picture. I have always sensed God's presence through nature, and I believe He speaks to us through His good creation, using it to lead us by still waters and restore our souls.

Soon after our arrival, the director of the internship program asked if we were ready to "go on the journey." I said, "Sure," without really understanding the ramifications of the question, not grasping the hard work that needed to be done on my soul. I was attracted to the program primarily because of the

> "That is my prayer for this year—that God will restore my soul."
>
> ***January 5, 2004***

opportunity to work in that innovative ministry environment while attending seminary. The spiritual formation component, the process of becoming more like Christ, was seen as an added bonus. However, I soon realized that this might actually be the primary reason that God called me here.

In a staff gathering one morning, a teaching pastor asked rhetorically, "Do you love Jesus, or just love talking about him?" That question hung in the air, and I suspect it lodged in the hearts of more than one pastor in the room. Loving Jesus and loving a ministry career are not necessarily the same thing. If you are a gifted communicator or leader, you can, by all outward appearances, be successful in ministry even as your relationship with God is stagnant. I think that is especially true in a high-pressure environment where we were expected to do everything with excellence and on a large scale. It's possible to rely on your talent and hard work, faking it for as long as possible. However, a ministry like that will eventually end badly—in burnout or, as we've seen this on far too many occasions, in scandal. The journey I had been invited to be, in part, meant to prevent that scenario.

A critical part of this spiritual formation journey was to really understand myself, my motivations, my brokenness, and my desires so that I could live out my calling from a healthy place. One of the first issues I needed to reconcile was my desire for approval. This is not, in itself, an unusual human desire; we all want to be valued and liked by others. However, for pastors, it is a potentially lethal desire. How exhausting must be the need for constant approval from the congregation, living or dying on the comments about your latest sermon. When a person is insecure in their relationship with God, they too often try to fill that hole with the adulation of the crowd. They become addicted to the adrenaline of approval and are crushed by criticism. The approval treadmill also harms the church, because the pastor who feeds on the approval of the crowd tells them only what they want to hear. This pastor is afraid to preach on challenging texts or lead change that might push the congregation beyond their comfort zones. Sadly, the greatest fear of many pastors is the disapproval of their own congregations.

As I looked at myself, I could see how the approval of others was more important for me than it should be. In this world of Christian celebrities where I was serving, I felt the need to be noticed and recognized as a leader. At the church, we emphasized the importance of living out of your spiritual gifts. However, there was no mistaking that the culture valued the gift of leadership above all the others. I knew I was a leader, but I wanted to lead from a healthy place. I wanted to break out of the approval trap and be more like the apostle Paul, who wrote what has become my life verse: "Am I now trying to win the approval of human beings, or of God? Or am I trying to please people? If I were still trying to please people, I would not be a servant of Christ." (Gal. 1:10)

A Mentor

As I began to peel back the layers of my story, it became clear that much of my need for approval came from my relationship with my father. The truth is, we are all wounded by our parents in some way, and we, in turn, all wound our children. My theory is that we should at least strive to pass on to our children junk that is different from the junk that was given to us by our parents. As I said, I have absolutely no doubt that my father loved me, but he had a hard time saying it. In fact, I can't remember him ever saying it to me. I knew it, but I needed to hear it.

Chapter Five

I have fond memories of us spending time together, but these were too few and far between. He traveled by car for his work and spent a lot of time driving on rural roads. He knew I loved animals. At one stage as a little boy, I was fascinated by turtles, so my dad would occasionally come home with a turtle he had seen crossing the road. I would keep it as a pet for a few days and then release it at a nearby lake. Once he even came home with a puppy. Now that I am a dad, I can see that on those long drives for work, I was on his mind. He was so immersed in his work, trying to build his business, provide a great life for us, and probably get the approval of his father. So, quite naturally, I transferred that need for his approval to others.

I was an only child and spent a great deal of time with my mom. There was never a moment's doubt about her unshakable faith or her love for me. She regularly told me she loved me, and she always modeled unconditional love. She also lived with a lot of fear that something tragic, such as an accident, would happen to my father or me. I think that came from the loss of her infant brother and from having too much responsibility as the eldest child, caring for her siblings while her parents were away at work. I was blessed with a happy childhood, but in some ways, I was emotionally trapped between a mom who continually expressed her anxiety and a father who almost never showed emotion. What I took away from that as a child was that the world is a scary place, but it is best to stuff your fears and emotions inside.

What does any of this have to do with my relationship with God or hearing His voice? The reality is that we hear God's voice through the filters of our own stories. If we don't do the hard work of unpacking our stories, the sound of God's voice will be distorted by our life experiences. Our emotional health is interwoven with our spiritual health, and that was a critical part of this journey I was on. My mentor and the director of the internship, Sheryl, carefully listened to my story and helped me to see the parts that were broken, which I could never have recognized on my own. She helped me see how that brokenness could be restored through Christ. She said that we grow when we meet God in "undefended vulnerability." That was a posture I had long avoided. My story had communicated to me that vulnerability was not good, tears were to be avoided, and emotions should be hidden.

I began to recognize how my story had impacted my relationship with God. It is why when I was first confronted with Brock's birth defects, my initial reaction was, "God, you are not going to push me away." Even now, as I am teased by colleagues about the brevity of my prayers, I know that pattern stems from an assumption that my heavenly Father is busy and has limited time for me. This hard journey of understanding myself allowed me to begin to see the truth, that the pain of my story was not an effort by God to push me away. It was actually to draw me near.

> **"It makes me think about God and suffering and grace and the long and winding road to here."**
> **February 8, 2004**

Somewhere along the way, I internalized a voice that said, "You are on your own." Maybe that is typical of an only child. I kept an emotional distance from God and from others. It created a vicious relational cycle. Through my poker face and lack of emotion, I communicated that I did not want or need to connect at a deep level. When others then responded by giving me space, I felt rejected. I was essentially "hiding from love," as author John Townsend

> **"I really feel isolated, probably because I don't let anyone in."**
> **January 10, 2004**

Chapter Five

describes in his book of that title.[10] This realization was a hard but essential truth. As time went by, my eyes were opened, and some tears began to flow. I could see how God was working in and through the experiences of my life to draw me closer to Him and reflect His love to others. It gave me a foundation to do ministry from a place of desire instead of from obligation or need.

Desire that is formed by Christ is essential for an abundant life. Many of us live with the notion that God is going to ask us to do something we don't want to do. I think that is why we sometimes keep our distance. However, what I discovered is that when we are really seeking His will, He doesn't ask us to do something we don't want to do; He changes our desires. As we grow in our relationship with Him, we essentially want what He wants. That's part of what it means to have the mind of Christ. He did not force me to leave the business world for ministry, to leave my home for Chicago, or even to attend seminary. He created in me a desire to let those things go in exchange for, as Paul described, the "surpassing worth of knowing Christ Jesus" (Phil. 3:8). That desire was to make knowing Him the center of my life.

The church's vision was to "turn irreligious people into fully devoted followers of Christ." It was, as described by the senior pastor, a "white-hot vision" that inspired the church. It was an intense, all consuming, results-based culture, and the results were undeniable. As many as twenty thousand people attended the services each weekend. On a weekly basis, I saw people's lives changed. I had never experienced a congregation where people were so committed to Christ and sharing Him with the world, nor have I since. It was a great atmosphere in which

---

10 John Townsend, *Hiding from Love: How to Change the Withdrawal Patterns That Isolate and Imprison You* (Grand Rapids, MI: Zondervan, 1996).

to learn and grow. I felt as if I were drinking from a fire hose, making up for lost time and gaining invaluable ministry experience. It was exhilarating, inspiring, and ultimately exhausting.

Each day began with a couple of hours of caffeine and seminary work before I headed to the church. In those days, my mind was filled either with some theological issue that had been deconstructed, and I was now trying to put back together, or a messy part of my story that needed to be unpacked. It was a lot to process, especially in a ministry environment that had a very different set of priorities. I was spending untold hours each week on theological education while I was working at a church that thought it was unnecessary. I was immersed in the life of the mind, while the internship culture told me I needed to get out of my head and crack open my heart. The deeper spiritual journey told me that my relationship with God was not dependent on my performance, while the church where I served told me "lost people mattered to God" and their eternal future was determined in large part by our hard work. In many ways, the more I grew in each of those aspects, the more my life became one of contradictions.

FOR REFLECTION

Take a few minutes to journal in response to these questions:

- ▶ When have you had a season of questioning your beliefs? What was that experience like? Did it happen in community or isolation?
- ▶ In what ways does the need for the approval of others impact your life?
- ▶ Do you think the filter of your story impacts how you view God? If so, how?

CHAPTER SIX

A Speaker, a Meeting, and a Padfolio (Rebecca)

> *This is what the LORD Almighty, the God of Israel, says to all those I carried into exile from Jerusalem to Babylon: "Build houses and settle down; plant gardens and eat what they produce. Marry and have sons and daughters; find wives for your sons and give your daughters in marriage, so that they too may have sons and daughters. Increase in number there; do not decrease. Also, seek the peace and prosperity of the city to which I have carried you into exile. Pray to the LORD for it, because if it prospers, you too will prosper."*
>
> —JEREMIAH 29:4–7

When we left home to move to Chicago, it felt as if all of my deep Southern roots were being severed. When we arrived in the Midwest, we didn't know a soul who lived there. It honestly felt as if I had been carried into exile, just as the Israelites had. Eugene Peterson, in his book *Run with the Horses*, described how I was feeling. He said, "The essential meaning of exile is that we are where we don't want to be.

We are separated from home."[11] I was overwhelmed by this new life in front of me. It was a relational blank slate that I had never experienced before. I looked at people differently—more deeply, more longingly. Wondering with each passing hello or short conversation if that person might become my friend. Surely, I could find a few friends who would help me hang on for the next three years.

Thankfully, many of our South Carolina friends and family came for visits. We were dying to see each one of them, but we hosted about every other weekend for the first year. I felt like a hotel maid and chef, washing sheets, flipping beds, and fixing meals in our small rental house that fit our family but was not big enough for many others. Everyone wanted to tour Chicago, take the train, eat out, shop, and enjoy the river tour of Lake Michigan. These visits were bittersweet. They took a large toll on me emotionally, physically, and financially, and we didn't have extra money to spend. Honestly, even as those visits were happening, I was depressed. It was hard to let go of everything I knew and start over, and then to have to say goodbye again and again one weekend after another. The root cutting was painful.

Sheryl, the internship director, told Jay that not all of our former friends would go on this journey with us. She said that a few would join us, and that God would add others along the way. She was so right. It was heartbreaking to lose some of our old friendships that meant the world to us. I had to grieve those unexpected losses, but I also celebrated the new friendships that came with the transition.

Most of the interns were in a much younger life stage, so we were deeply grateful to God that Barry and Lori, a couple from Texas with whom we connected during the initial internship retreat, decided

---

11 Eugene Peterson, *Run with the Horses: The Quest for Life at Its Best* (Downers Grove, IL: IVP, 2019).

to move to Chicago too. Their son and daughter were about the age of our children. Like us, they had jumped off the business-world cliff midlife because they felt God's call to pursue full-time ministry. We were thankful to be with people who truly understood what this life of surrender felt like. Don't get me wrong, it wasn't a surrendered life of attending to the dying like Mother Theresa in Calcutta, or moving to a jungle to be missionaries, but we four had surrendered to being willing to do whatever God wanted us to do with our lives. *Whatever* is a hard posture to be in.

We bonded with this couple quickly. Both Barry and Jay worked at the same church, studied mind-numbing theology with six-hundred-page books like *The Hermeneutical Spiral*,[12] questioned what they had gotten themselves into, and pondered what their futures might look like. Meanwhile, Lori and I talked, cried, laughed, and prayed as we walked the journey together. We shared ordinary meals and holiday meals when we couldn't go home to be with our extended families. Thankfully, Lori loved to cook, which is my least favorite thing to do, and I got to add my touch to the festivities by setting tables with candles and beautiful wildflowers and weeds I had picked from the edges of the winding trails in our neighborhood.

I lived in pity-party mode for about a year, and then I decided to fully invest myself in our new life. I am not sure what made me flip the switch, but a year seemed long enough to wallow in the homesickness and sadness. Eugene Peterson also wrote these

"I needed to turn the corner and make this home for the sake of my sanity, my family, and for establishing new relationships."

November 2004

---

12 Grant R. Osborne, *The Hermeneutical Spiral: A Comprehensive Introduction to Biblical Interpretation* (Downers Grove, IL: IVP, 2006).

words about someone in exile: "The aim of the person of faith is not to be as comfortable as possible but to live as deeply and thoroughly as possible—to deal with the reality of life, discover truth, create beauty and act out love."[13] It was time for me to turn outward and live deeply.

While there was something sad about starting all new friendships from scratch, it was also exciting to see whom God placed on my path and how He might weave those relationships together. One afternoon, while I was at the elementary school's playground with William, I met a mother and her son. Much like the way I blurted out to the woman with the baby at McDonald's, I found myself saying to this mom, "We just moved here, and I don't know anybody!" That one conversation led to many more. It was the beginning of a deep and sweet neighborhood friendship between two moms and two sons who became best friends. We invited their family to church, and they began to go with us. Almost weekly, on Saturday nights we would drive our minivan to their home just half a block from our house, they would pile in, and off we would go for the fifteen-minute ride to church, chatting it up all the way there.

In addition to missing our people back home, we also missed our family hobby: Clemson football. We sold our season football tickets, but we continued to pay our annual fees to keep our seats reserved for the seasons to come. During the first fall season away from the South, we were excited to watch the season opener, Clemson versus Alabama. We signed a contract with Direct TV to get satellite access. We almost tore up our rental house getting it installed and connected to two TVs, but we didn't care. We had to be able to watch, even if it was remotely. As game time was nearing, our family piled on the couch in all our orange gear and turned on the TV, only to find out that this game was blacked

---

13 Peterson, *Horses*, 148.

out in our area. It was another sour reminder of being away from home and the things we loved.

As our relationships continued to expand, Jay and I began to be tapped for all kinds of things by our neighbors—advice, marriage counseling, and childcare. I even watched two small children overnight for a mom who went to the hospital to have a baby. I barely knew her. I was surprised to see how few genuine friendships people had. Because we were nice, friendly, and desired relationships, many of our neighbors quickly gravitated toward us.

As we settled into our new life, I had no idea that I was called to anything except to support Jay in his work and to be his editor-in-chief for his seminary papers. I was not qualified to edit theology, but I would do my best to read, review, and often comment, "I don't know what you are talking about here, but you do need a comma right there." My other roles as a stay-at-home mom and Chicago tour guide continued. However, when I read *Power of a Praying Wife* back in 2003, there were some words that were captured in my heart: "God has called *you* to something, too. But it will fit in with whatever your husband's calling is, it will not be in conflict with it. . . . The timing to do what God has called *each* of you to do will work out perfectly, if it's submitted to God."[14]

> "Beyond mother/wife/ maid/cook, who am I? Why am I?"
>
> May 2005

A Speaker

One of the best parts of the internship was that I was privileged to serve at and attend the amazing church conferences hosted throughout the year on the main campus in Barrington, Illinois. I, too, was getting a spiritual MBA, as the who's who of national and international church

---

14 Omartian, *Power of a Praying Wife*, 95.

leaders spoke at these conferences. The annual conferences included ones for small groups, evangelism, the prevailing church, the arts, teaching, and the leadership summit, to name a few. I was like a sponge, soaking in as much as I could from each speaker and song.

During one of the small group conferences, I heard a speaker named Dan Allender, a professor of counseling psychology and president of the Seattle School of Theology and Psychology in Washington. I still remember the exact spot where I was sitting that day at the conference. I was serving as a greeter, so I was in a single chair between the entry doors to the church's lakeside auditorium. The conference was held in the same space I had been in months prior for Vision Night. These are the words Dan spoke: "Your whole story matters to God." At that moment, something deep inside me shifted. My *whole* story matters? Even the dark and ugly parts? The parts buried deep in my soul? Is it possible that those parts matter to God? It was an awakening. It was a new vision for me—a mixture of deep insight into my story, my connection with God, my heart and my soul.

It was such a startling awakening that I purchased a copy of Allender's book *To Be Told*[15] in order to read, digest, and process what he had said. I began to dig into and reflect on my full life story. I wrote much of it out on paper, with a trail of tears as I journaled the details. I had the opportunity to share the highs and the lows of my story verbally with a small circle of friends. I began to wrestle with the harder parts of my story. I even signed up for a six-week class to bring into the light an especially dark and dreary part of my story that happened in college.

One evening during those painful six weeks, Jay and I attended a mid-week service where the senior pastor was teaching on Psalm 51,

---

15 Dan Allender, *To Be Told: Know Your Story, Shape Your Future* (Colorado Springs, CO: WaterBrook, 2009).

about David's anguish over his adultery with Bathsheba. As he spoke, he said that we need to admit that we have sinned, agree that we have done evil in God's sight, and ask God if He will wash us. During that evening, those words pierced my heart, tears streamed down my cheeks, and the darkness and heaviness of that part of my story was washed as white as snow. I was able to forgive and fully accept that I was forgiven as well. The deep pain and sorrow felt on and off through the years felt as if it had been taken away from me that night, and it has never returned.

Throughout this time of processing my story, I was thinking how great it was to have this time in Chicago to work on my story with God and others, and to deal with it while far away from South Carolina. I could leave my emotional baggage in Chicago and not have to carry it elsewhere or share it with friends and family back home. But as always, God had a bigger plan.

I had heard the word *redemption* many times, but I had never experienced it. I had never fully understood what it meant. On two separate occasions, I felt prompted to share the hard part of my college story: once, with a mere acquaintance at a women's retreat, and another time with a friend. My story struck them deep in their stories. In fact, both of them almost yelled out loud when I told them. My words connected to their souls so much that it hurt. Over time, it helped them to begin to work through the dark areas of their stories and expose them to the light. That's what redemption is: God using all the parts of our stories, both good and bad, to bring healing and restoration to others in the world.

A Meeting

At this point, I felt overwhelmed by my new life in Chicago. I had quickly turned from depressed and disengaged to fully invested, so much so that I was inundated with other people's needs while trying to maintain family connections and friendships back home, make new friends, raise my kids, welcome visitors, and keep all the plates spinning.

Jay suggested that I was building into so many people that I needed to have someone to invest in me. He suggested that I contact a woman on staff at the church named Sibyl. For days, I talked myself out of reaching out for help. One day, Jay called and said that he was praying for me, and he didn't want me to dismiss the idea.

That gave me the courage to email Sibyl. She emailed back to say that she would meet with me. In her email, I noticed her title: director of spiritual mentoring. I had no idea that I had gone straight to the top for this initial conversation. We had a meeting at a table in the middle of the church's cafeteria. I shared with her a bit of my story, how I was investing in others in my neighborhood, how I was handling being a mom, as well as how stressed I felt. She listened carefully, or at least, I thought she did. I honestly thought the next step would be that she would connect me to a mentor in her network. Instead, within a week of our first meeting, she emailed to tell me that she was working on a project with her friend Sharon, and she asked if I would be interested in meeting with them.

Had she heard a word I said? I didn't need a project. I was overwhelmed, and I had enough projects of my own.

Since Jay had sparked this relationship, he didn't discourage me. So, despite my weariness, I decided to attend the meeting to scope it out. We met in yet another conference room. As Sibyl and Sharon described their dream, vision, and project, they told me they wanted to write a book with visual maps that would help individuals to process their life stories: past, present, future—the good and the bad. I was excited and nervous.

I couldn't believe that I was being asked to be on the ground floor of such an amazing project. It connected to my own story work as well as to the healing and redemption I had experienced in the prior months. It dawned on me that during our first meeting, Sibyl must have been listening to me with one ear and to God with the other. He apparently was whispering to her to invite me to join their team. How could I possibly turn this opportunity down? Without hesitation or prayer, I jumped on board.

That project was a labor of love, blood, sweat, tears, and prayers. We took what was in their hearts and minds and began to put it on paper. As each section was developed, we worked with a graphic artist in California to create visual maps to accompany their words. It was a sheer joy to work with Sibyl and Sharon week in and week out, as this project morphed from concept to reality. The final outcome was the development of *Listen to My Life: Maps for Recognizing and Responding to God in My Story*.[16] I touched every detail of the content, editing, publishing, printing, distribution, and website development for the material. I literally collated and shipped the material from my dining room table. I even learned just enough about HTML to keep the website up to date along the way.

We also developed and implemented class, retreat, and workshop plans to help people engage with their stories. I experienced the thrill of traveling and teaching alongside them at retreats and classes. I believe without a doubt that this was the reason God called *me* to Chicago, and it was the beginning of my call into ministry to help connect people to God. The work stretched me mentally with website development and project management, and it stretched me spiritually as I got to work and experience life each week with women of deep faith. Their investment in

---

16 Listen to My Life, https://www.onelifemaps.com (Bartlett, IL: 2019).

me and our investment in that project together grew me in ways I never could have imagined. I think I won the spiritual life lottery with the gift of those amazing years. God really had called me to something too, and it fit perfectly with Jay's calling.

A Padfolio

One of our Listen to My Life retreats was held at a beautiful corporate office with large glass windows overlooking the skyline of Dallas. I hadn't been in a corporate setting in any official capacity since my IBM days of long ago. As Sibyl, Sharon, and I got off the elevator on the ninth floor, we were welcomed by the hosts. I was given my name tag and a black padfolio (a portable case that opens like a book to hold an eight-and-a-half-by-eleven-inch notepad) with the logo of Leadership Network, the Christian organization that was hosting us.

As soon as they handed it to me, I was in shock. I could have crawled into a corner and wept. I had carried a leather one similar to it during the days of my eleven-year career with IBM. It was a visible, physical representation of the culmination of God's work in my life to date. God had taken my corporate experience, the good and bad parts of my story, my ability to organize and accomplish a multitude of different types of tasks, and my spiritual growth, and then He tied it all together for His purposes. While those thoughts were spinning around in my head, I pulled myself back together, wiped my tears, and turned my attention toward orchestrating a retreat for thirty women that had flown in from all over the country. The retreat was so well received that we were invited back to facilitate future women's retreats.

When I had time to journal and process what had happened that day, I realized that I had to let go of my ordinary life in South Carolina

Chapter Six

to be a part of something extraordinary. I had to be willing to let go in order to receive what God had planned for me.

While I continued my work on Listen to My Life, the church decided to take steps toward the launch of a neighborhood ministry, and they asked Jay and me to be a part of a pilot. They gave us a list of approximately ten families who were members and lived in our neighborhood. We were surprised and excited to see all the names on the list. We received no other official instructions, so we began to invite them over so we could get to know one another and dream and pray about how God might use us to love each other and our neighborhood. Friendships began to develop within that group. We started hosting neighborhood gatherings such as picnics, Easter egg hunts, and Halloween chili dinners. Each year in December, our favorite annual event was a progressive dinner.

We also hosted neighborhood Bible studies and monthly dinners. Through these activities, my friendships deepened, and I decided to be brave and ask one friend to join me for a Listen to My Life neighborhood group. She said yes, and so did seven others. For a year, we came together once or twice a month to share. As we shared about our histories, our current lives, and our desires and hopes for the future, we often used pictures and objects to help describe the situations along with our thoughts and feelings. When I described my personal desires, I brought a large red marble heart to signify that I wanted God to soften my heart. I wanted to love more and feel more loved. I also brought a $2 bill to represent my desire for a better relationship with money. I wanted to see money as a tool, not as a way to define success. We got to know each other deeply—the good, the broken, the sin—and we prayed each other through. It was frightening and glorious all at the same time. They each became such sweet, deep, soulful friends. Because of my experiences leading that group of neighborhood women, I was able to write a group guide for Listen to My Life for others to use in their communities.

One of these friends shared that her wedding and celebration was very small when she was married, so when her twenty-fifth anniversary rolled around, we hosted a large neighborhood dinner gathering with a beautiful, white, multi-tiered wedding cake for dessert. What a joy it was to know their story and celebrate them!

We were able to see God at work among the church members as spiritual friendships began to form, and deepening friendships and conversations happened among families scattered throughout the neighborhood. It was a beautiful view of what God can do with a little effort on the part of those willing to love one another. I haven't experienced that many deep friendships within one neighborhood before or since. It was a moment in time that God had prepared for us. Many of those sweet friends have now moved to other states. And we all have taken that beautiful experience with us to our new homes and neighborhoods.

Throughout this time, I attended women's Bible studies, and I was also able to attend women's retreats. Again, it was like more classes toward my spiritual MBA—a concentrated time of processing my story, listening for God, and learning from the best, including John Ortberg, who taught us on Wednesday nights during our church's mid-week gatherings. John left the church soon after we arrived, but Jay and I continued to make the mid-week church gathering our date night each week no matter who was teaching. Even when snow was covering the roads, out the door we Southerners would go, slipping and sliding as we drove the seven-mile trek to church.

Chapter Six

As we were rounding out our second year in Chicago, we began to have serious questions about what was next. Jay had been asked to consider taking a full-time paid staff role as an area pastor at the church. That idea felt daunting. What I had originally signed up for was a three-year internship. We had no idea what the future would look like, but home and family were still calling my name. Several people suggested that we attend one of the monthly elder prayer sessions after the service for guidance and wisdom. I didn't think our need was big enough, but we felt prompted to go. Jay and I waited in line for an elder, and she asked, "Why are you here?" We told her that we had a major decision to make regarding our next steps with the internship. She prayed that we would have a telescopic and microscopic vision. Not really sure what that meant other than thinking about it through our current situation and the future potential, we attended again the next month, and two elders prayed over us. They asked that God would in some way paint a billboard. Yes, a billboard, just as I had prayed for when I was seeking discernment for surgery for Neale. Goosebumps. They prayed about landscaping a yard and knowing where to plant things. What an odd thing to pray for!

The next day, I sat down in my beloved red chaise lounge chair in my bedroom and decided to reread Jeremiah 29 from the beginning. Jeremiah 29:5 says, "Build houses and settle down; plant gardens." "Oh no!" I yelled out loud as I read this text. It sounded as if God was speaking to me again. Again, it was not audible, but a deep nudging in my spirit. And it seemed that He was suggesting that we should let our shallow roots grow deeper here. It was not what I wanted to hear.

Jay felt as if he was still in a time of preparation. I think he felt he needed to learn more, lead more, and experience more before he took another big step. He suggested that if we were owners of a house rather than tenants, that might help us feel more settled. That was a nerve-racking idea, as I had only made a short-term commitment to this life in Chicago, not an indefinite one. We talked with our children about their desires, and we all discussed a picture of our preferences in a house. That weekend, we began to look at homes in the same neighborhood as our rental home and the place where we had connected with our neighbors. Our mouths dropped wide open when we walked into the second house on our real estate tour. It had everything on our wish list, including a massive backyard, a wooden playground with three swings and a slide, a large kitchen with an island for extra seating, an extra bedroom for guests, an office area for me, and a small playroom for the kids. As I looked around at each square foot, I could envision all of our furniture in storage back home fitting in each space perfectly. However, Jay hadn't officially been offered any church staff role, and we weren't even sure we wanted him to have the job.

> **"I'm just really sad right now. We are staying here—a place that is not my home. Walk through the sadness with me so that I can get to the other side of it."**
>
> **October 2005**

We knew that we would have, at a minimum, one more year in Chicago. We loved the house so much that we made a thirty-day contingency offer on it. My feelings were so mixed up. The two years had turned into a blessing, but I still missed my family, my friends, my home, Clemson football games, and the beach. Even though I felt fully invested in this new life, I had bouts of sadness and continually had to renew my decision to invest in the daily life God had put on the path before us. However, the path now seemed to be stretching out longer than I was prepared to travel.

Chapter Six

In that thirty-day window, our rental home was placed under contract for purchase by another couple in the internship. That allowed us to be released from our lease, which would enable us to move forward on the potential purchase of this house. What were we thinking?

During that time, with my neighborhood friends, I attended a retreat in Wisconsin for the women of the church called SoulFeast. We learned about spiritual practices. (I honestly had never heard that term before.) I attended the session on the practice of solitude. The teaching was powerful, and I was so impacted by it that I scheduled solitude on my calendar from that point forward, once a month from 9:00 a.m. to 2:00 p.m., while my children were in school. I would read, journal, walk, pray, and nap. I believe those hours in solitude and all the other experiences during our time in Chicago were a time of preparation for my future.

At the end of the solitude teaching session at that retreat, the Lord's Supper was offered. Sitting next to me was the person who was leaving the staff position for which Jay was being considered. She washed my hands and served me the Communion elements. It felt as if she was passing the torch to us.

FOR REFLECTION

Take a few minutes to journal in response to these questions:

- ▶ Where have you experienced redemption—God using the good and bad parts of your story to bring healing and restoration to others?
- ▶ Rebecca writes, "I had to be willing to let go in order to receive." Where have you experienced this to be true in your own life?
- ▶ What meeting or conversation have you had that changed the trajectory of your life? Do you think God directed you to it?
- ▶ Rebecca shares how her need for support prompted her initial meeting with Sibyl, which led to her calling in Chicago. When have you experienced God taking a need in your life and transforming it into a calling?

CHAPTER SEVEN

A Monet Painting, a Bombing, and a Dangerous Trip (Jay)

> *"The Spirit of the Lord is on me, because he has anointed me to proclaim good news to the poor. He has sent me to proclaim freedom for the prisoners and recovery of sight for the blind, to set the oppressed free, to proclaim the year of the Lord's favor."*
>
> —Luke 4:18–19

There was one question family and friends from home continued to ask: "When are you coming back?" It was, in all honesty, an annoying question. On the one hand, I appreciated their desire for us to return and pick up where we left off. On the other hand, it seemed disconnected from the reality of our present lives and how we had experienced our sense of calling. I hadn't moved to Chicago to escape friends and family. I didn't see whatever was next as simply a job relocation, but as another time during which we needed to know that God was leading us. In retrospect, I think there was another reason the question annoyed me. Deep down, even if I would not say it aloud, it's what I hoped for as well. In fact, with one more year remaining in the internship program, I wrote in my journal that what I really desired was "to have my old life back and do ministry at a high level."

I was in a strange place in more ways than one. I had one year remaining in the internship program, but because of my decision to pursue a MDiv, I had two years remaining in seminary. I had transitioned from evangelism ministry, where I had worked with those exploring or new to the Christian faith, to the newly launched neighborhood ministry. Rebecca and I were inspired by our experience in our own neighborhood community and felt as if this was the best way to serve in what we assumed was my final year at the church. I loved the emerging vision of living out the gospel in our communities instead of just trying to attract people to attend church services. It fit with the more holistic sense of the gospel that I had begun to embrace through a shift in my own theological perspective. When I arrived, I was focused on getting people to heaven, but now, more and more, I was drawn to the idea of getting heaven into people.

When I shifted to neighborhood ministry, I saw it as an opportunity to serve in an area of passion and learn more before my time at the church ended. However, soon after my arrival, things began to shift in a dramatic way. I was approached about the possibility of leaving the internship early to serve as full-time staff in the role of area pastor, as Rebecca mentioned earlier. It was a great ministry opportunity that had opened because the area pastor for Barrington decided to leave her position to lead a local nonprofit. At this time, the church had divided up ministry by geography. The job would include responsibility for pastoral care, community life, compassion, and justice for one of the largest areas within the geographical footprint of the church. It was also the area where the main church campus was located and most of the

Chapter Seven

senior leaders lived. So, in essence, I would be going from the relative anonymity of the internship to a high-pressure role where everything I did would be very visible.

It forced me to once again wrestle with my desire to return home. Making the decision to move forward with this position meant making a long-term commitment to stay in Chicago. I felt as if the role fit me, and I was excited about the vision. My questions were about staying in Chicago and my work-life balance. For the past two years, the journey had taught me the importance of living out of my relationship with God, not my performance for God. Did I want to end my internship experience at a more life-giving rhythm or amp up the pace and expectations? After all, I still had two years remaining in seminary. Could I handle this role and seminary without sacrificing my relationships with my family and with God?

I did not know the answer to that question, but I felt that I should explore the possibility. The process took several months. During that time, I sought advice from a variety of voices who affirmed my fit for the position. I carved out time to listen for God's voice in solitude, and I did a lot of journaling. Taking time to write down my thoughts had become an important part of my spiritual journey. The act of putting pen to paper helped to clarify my thinking and allowed me to see patterns of how God was leading. In retrospect, it's such a gift to be able to look back and see in black and white how God answered our prayers. Without those journals, you would not be reading this book.

This felt like another critical decision for us, a hinge point in our story. We went to the church in Chicago with the clear intention to come back home as soon as I finished seminary. However, nothing I had experienced in the past two years pointed back to where we had begun.

I was on a steep spiritual growth curve and felt affirmed in ministry. I was excited about the vision and the opportunity to be a part of it, to continue to learn and to grow. Besides, I was not yet qualified for a role in my old Presbyterian context. I would need to complete my seminary degree for that. The church's leadership, on the other hand, did not care about a seminary degree; they just saw how I fit into their strategy and thought I could get results. I was passionate about the vision and trusted the leadership of Gene, the lead pastor who had arrived around the same time as we had. His arrival allowed the senior pastor to step back from leading the church and focus on inspiring local churches around the world, or so we thought at the time. I had gotten to know Gene, and I appreciated his passion for the church and his authenticity as a leader. I was excited about the possibility of being on his team.

After weeks of interviews and much prayer, in July 2005, I accepted the area pastor position, which of course included making a commitment to stay in Chicago. My thoughts of going home would have to go back on the shelf. We knew that our decision would be painful for our parents, but as always, they supported us and trusted in God's guidance in our lives. In fact, we decided to go ahead and buy the home we had found in the neighborhood. It gave us more room for our family, so it felt as if we were really settling in for the long haul. I was excited about the neighborhood focus. Some of it was based on a concept from Randy Frazee's book *Making Room for Life*.[17] In fact, the church recruited Randy to lead this new neighborhood effort. It was an exciting time, as it seemed that we had everything we needed to help make a huge ministry transition. We were not just going to focus on attracting people to come to weekend services, we would focus on serving and investing

---

17 Randy Frazee, *Making Room for Life: Trading Chaotic Lifestyles for Connected Relationships* (Grand Rapids, MI: Zondervan, 2003).

in the community in our neighborhoods. I loved the vision then, and I still love it all these years later.

A Monet Painting

Unfortunately, what began with so much enthusiasm and promise eventually would end in frustration and disillusion. I could write a book or create a podcast just on the experiences I had during those years. We used to joke that a year on staff during this period was like dog years; each one felt like seven. We launched the neighborhood ministry model with something called the Table, which was a gathering of church members for a meal in a home in their communities. It was these types of gatherings that would guide the people of the Chicago suburbs to live out the gospel. We imagined it as living out the vision of the early church where they gathered and broke bread and impacted their community (Acts 2:42–44). The weekend we launched, we had five hundred Table gatherings planned, and somewhere around seven thousand people participated. It was a massive undertaking, and overall, it was a great success that left all of us thoroughly exhausted.

The launch was soon followed by a retreat during which all the pastors were supposed to have the opportunity to recharge. The pastor scheduled to lead the retreat asked each person to bring a picture from their childhood. He wanted us to use these to share bits of our stories so we could get to know one another better and bond as a team. However, at the last minute he found he could not be there because of a family emergency. The overall leader of the neighborhood ministry took his place. He began the retreat by saying something to the effect of, "if you want to show

"I want to feel the natural flow of the seasons and not just a rush of meetings and chaos."

July 22, 2008

your picture to someone while on break that is fine, but we have a lot of work to do." Instead of a retreat for spiritual nourishment, it became a tension-filled offsite meeting that just increased the team's exhaustion and anxiety. This was a pattern that would play out time and time again. When something was successful, it only increased the visibility and the pressure for leaders to make it even bigger and better the next time.

The senior pastor was still in the picture, and when he turned up the heat, some leaders would melt, burning everyone around them. After all, he often explained that the stakes were "sky-high" and the church was "the hope of the world." There are several reasons that the neighborhood strategy ultimately failed, but most of them flowed from a toxic leadership culture. We were promoting the idea of making room for life, and at the same time, the staff was living in a culture of chaos and pressure. Essentially, we were selling something that we were not living.

In the years that followed, I began to see the church in Chicago as one sees a Monet painting. It appeared beautiful from a distance, but the closer you got to it, the more confused and disorienting it became. Amid the dysfunction, it was still a place God used in powerful ways. I saw many people come to Christ and live out their faith in their communities. I saw more people baptized in a weekend than many pastors see in a lifetime. These were not just statistics; they were real people whom I knew in personal ways. Those years showed me how God can change lives even amid the dysfunctional and difficult circumstances of the church.

The life change was real, and it all looked beautiful from across the room. However, as you drew closer and saw the

"I believe that it can be different—must be different. I don't want to settle for this."

September 19, 2008

staff culture, it became hard to reconcile. I went on staff believing that God did amazing things through this church because of its leadership. Within a few years, I concluded that God did amazing things through this church despite its leadership.

During those years, my seminary training moved toward its conclusion. I kept up the pace of studying early in the morning before going to the office and traveling to Bethel for more intensives. Those weeks at Bethel were challenging, as we essentially crammed a semester of lectures into a week. In late January, as I began my final semester, I went away for a day of solitude in a rural area not far from our home. Intentional times of solitude had become an important spiritual rhythm. I needed the opportunity to experience God's presence without the noise and accomplishment of ministry. During one of those weeks, I saw a tree that reminded me of the one I had seen in my first intensive at seminary four years earlier. This old tree had a big chunk of frozen snow that had settled into a crook. It appeared to be immovable, frozen there for the rest of the long winter. I sensed God saying through the image of that tree that as four years of theological education drew to a close, I had what I needed for the journey ahead. In those four years, some of my notions about God had fallen to the ground and blown away, but those had been replaced by fresh ideas that were stronger and more solidly settled. I felt that God had given me a picture of closure through His creation.

A Bombing

In the midst of all of the organizational frustrations, God was working to bring clarity to how I viewed the gospel and my place in it. One of the blessings of being on staff at the church was the opportunity to participate in experiences that expanded our view of

God's presence amid some of the injustices in the world. One of those experiences occurred for me in June 2007. I was invited to be a part of a justice journey, exploring the part that God calls us to play in racial reconciliation. We would travel throughout the South by bus with a group from an African American church in Chicago to visit places of significance in the civil rights struggle. During the week, we traveled to Selma, Birmingham, Atlanta, and Memphis. At the end of each day, we had the opportunity to process our experiences and perceptions together as a diverse community.

As someone who grew up in South Carolina during the civil rights struggle, the trip felt very personal. I vividly remember attending a county fair with my parents and having four members of the Ku Klux Klan sit down behind us in the grandstands. I remember the racism in my family and community. I vividly recall when I was in fourth grade and my school was integrated. I had an African American teacher that year, which was quite a shift in our paradigm. So, for me, this trip was an opportunity to relive some of those hard memories, reflecting on where I had come from and where I was going.

We had the privilege to share that trip with Dr. John Perkins, author of *One Blood*[18] and a giant in the struggle for racial reconciliation in the church. He shared his personal stories of being a part of the civil rights struggle, and he also taught us how the church should be the place of unity and reconciliation (2 Cor. 5:11–21). I remember he stated that being born again should be the last individualistic act of our lives.

The things we saw and heard that week were deeply impactful. That was especially true for me when we visited the 16th Street Baptist Church in Birmingham, the place where, in 1963, a Klan bombing killed

---

18 John M. Perkins, *One Blood: Parting Words to the Church on Race and Love* (Chicago: Moody, 2018)

four little girls as they were getting ready for their church Youth Day celebration. As we drove to the church, I saw the hotel where we had stayed when we came to Birmingham for Brock's surgery years earlier. As my mind relived the experience of losing our child, I heard the story of the loss of these four children. As we shared Communion in that church, I could imagine the anguish of those parents and the toll that racism had taken on all of our souls.

This was another time when I could glimpse God's providence. He knew I would be in this place at this time, and He was weaving it all together for a purpose I could not yet see. As we drove back to Chicago, I reflected on this in my journal. I wondered why He had taken me so far from home so I could return on a bus and finally see what I had missed for years. I sensed that my own justice journey was just beginning.

A Dangerous Trip

The next step in that journey occurred the following spring. I was invited to be a part of a vision trip to South Africa and Malawi. I had always wanted to go to Africa, and I jumped at the opportunity. The church in Chicago was heavily involved in ministering to those experiencing the HIV/AIDS crisis in southern Africa at a time when few churches were engaged in the issue. The situation in South Africa was dire, with one thousand people dying per day, leaving behind two and a half million orphans.

A few weeks before the trip, we were participating in a church-wide service project, packing hundreds of thousands of packages of meals for Africa. While at the event, I shared with a representative of the organization that I was leaving for Africa the following week. He asked where I was going. When I told him Malawi, he got a very serious look on his face and said, "That's a dangerous trip."

I was a little taken aback. He said, "Do you have all of your shots?"

I replied that I had all the recommended vaccinations.

He said, "Well, anyway, that's not why it's dangerous. It's dangerous because you will never be able to get those kids out of your mind."

Truer words were never spoken.

We traveled to South Africa and spent the first week visiting churches that were involved in the crisis. What we saw was heartbreaking. We visited child-headed households where older children cared for siblings, all of them orphaned by this terrible disease. We spent time with widows with several children, all of them HIV positive. It's a good thing that adoption was such a difficult process. Otherwise, I would have brought more than one child home with me.

While it was inspiring to see the local church serving these communities in crisis, there was no end to the heartbreak. I met with one pastor who told me that, in addition to everything else, he performed an average of seven funerals a week for people in his church who died from AIDS. It made my frustrations back in Chicago seem trivial.

We next traveled to Malawi, where the church was part of a child-survival program in a rural district called Chitipa. We flew in a small private plane and landed on an unlit dirt airstrip just before sundown. When we landed, hundreds of children swarmed the plane. These were the kids I had been warned about, the kids whom I would never be able to get out of my mind. I had learned over the past week that when I got around these large groups of children my eyes would fill with tears. Yet again, God was using the pain of my story to crack open my heart for the world. As we made our way to our lodging in the fading light, I saw an ox cart carrying a pregnant woman to the district hospital. I felt as if I had been transported to the first century.

We spent the next three days there seeing the impact of the local church in a place of desperate need. I loved the rural community and the warmth of the people. I remember watching kids playing with balls made with plastic bags tied together with banana fibers, or rolling an old tire down a road. They wore dirty t-shirts with logos from America. They had no shoes, but what they did have was huge smiles and laughter, an innocent joy that we don't often see in our world of plenty. I would take their pictures and then show them on my digital camera. They would all howl with laughter at seeing their images. Another would then say, "Snap me," and it would repeat all over again.

The poverty was shocking, but at the same time it seemed hopeful, because unlike the townships in South Africa, which were filled with racial tension and violence, the community in rural Malawi was still intact. As our plane took off to a waving throng of children, I had no idea that this was just the first of many, many visits to this beautiful place and these people in the warm heart of Africa.

We returned to South Africa and had one more day to visit projects around Johannesburg. On our way to visit a church, their pastor called to ask if we could instead meet him at the hospital. He was headed there to visit a ten-year-old boy who was dying of AIDS. The pastor felt that this would give us a clearer picture than would a visit to the church. The last place I wanted to go was a ward filled with dying children. In fact, I remember standing in the parking lot outside the hospital and trying to think of an excuse to avoid going inside.

Breathless Haste

There was no food for the moms at the hospital, so they made their own meals outside. We walked past them and into the ward filled with their sick kids. We gathered around this gaunt ten-year-old and his mother, and we prayed for them. We prayed that God would do something miraculous, as I knew from experience that He could. When we walked out, our group was emotionally drained. We drove in silence for quite some time, lost in the pain we had seen in the face of that little boy.

Someone asked Rebecca why the church wanted me to go on that trip. Her response was, "To break his heart so that he will do something about it." In that respect, it was a success on all counts. God was taking me beyond my comfort zone and connecting the pain of the world with the pain of my own story. He was using these experiences to change my heart, my perspective on ministry, and eventually the lives of some of those children I could not get out of my mind.

FOR REFLECTION

Take a few minutes to journal in response to these questions:

▶ Do you struggle to keep your focus on your relationship with God instead of your performance for God? What helps you from falling into the performance trap?

▶ Have you ever experienced tension and frustration in the church? If so, how do you differentiate your relationship with God from the church as an institution?

▶ How has God used the pain in your story to crack open your heart for the world?

CHAPTER EIGHT

A Little Boy, Breathless Haste, and a Scrapbook (Rebecca)

> I will stand at my post,
> I will take up my position on the watch-tower,
> I will watch to learn what [God] will say through me,
> and what I shall reply when I am challenged.
>
> Then the LORD made answer:
> Write down the vision, inscribe it on tablets,
> ready for a herald to carry it with speed;
> for there is still a vision for the appointed time.
> At the destined hour it will come in
> breathless haste, *it will not fail.*
> If it delays, wait for it;
> for when it comes will be no time to linger.
>
> The reckless will be unsure of himself,
> while the righteous man will live by being faithful . . .
>
> —HABAKKUK 2:1–4, NEB (emphasis added)

Ours two annual vacations both revolved around going back to South Carolina to see friends and family. We spent much of the time making the thirteen-hour drive back home and then being pulled from place to place to be able to see everyone in the course of a week. It never felt like a restful vacation. I would see family for short stints of time and grieve as we said goodbye. At the end of one such trip, we were leaving, and I said, "I don't want to go back to Chicago!" The years we had been given there had provided life-changing experiences, spiritual training, and more opportunities than we could ask for or imagine, and we both loved our work. However, I still deeply yearned for home. I didn't know how many more times I could say goodbye to the people I loved the most, but we continued to do it time after time.

Jay and I talked about an exit strategy, as if we were in charge of our own timetable. We agreed to one more year, which gave me a little relief. At that point, the children would be going into fifth grade and eighth grade,

> "God, are you working/preparing my heart for whatever is next? I know you are, but is it a BIG next?"
>
> September 26, 2008

which would be a great setup for them to get to know friends before they entered middle school and high school. A few months later, my neighborhood friends took me out for my birthday, and I had the sense that it would be my last birthday there.

A Little Boy

Jay's passion for Africa continued to grow. When he returned from his first trip, he shared stories with me that would tug at my heart. One of these was a picture of a little boy with a ragged orange shirt. The back of his shirt was completely missing, and the front was held together by only the collar around his neck. He was holding two handmade balls

Chapter Eight

made of old, dirty plastic bags with string tightly wound around them to help keep their form.

A few months later, Neale joined a travel softball team. She had discovered her love for this sport following our arrival in Chicago. She declared to her father one day that she wanted to be a pitcher. Day in, day out, she would pitch to Jay beside our rental house. His hours of sitting on the ball bucket catching for her are some of his fondest memories, and it allowed for some of their best conversations. Pitching lessons and hours of practice as a pitcher and first baseman on other teams helped her to secure a spot on this travel team. The coaches asked us to raise money for her team so each player could have two uniforms with their name and number on the hat, batting bag, and jersey.

Not long after Neale joined the travel team, we had dinner with one of the church's African mission partners. She lived in Malawi, and she was supported by our church to attend to the many needs of the people in that country. She had hosted Jay and the vision team while they were there. During our conversation, I chatted about how my daughter had made the team and that we now had to raise money for her.

She asked, "How much money?"

I could hardly speak. I wanted to throw up. "A thousand dollars," I said.

A week or two later, it was nine-year-old William's football "homecoming" weekend. He wore a new, clean, and crisp navy and gold uniform with his name on the back of his jersey. The parents brought paint to decorate the cars, team tattoos for our faces, matching scarves for each mom, and cowbells painted with the team logo. We then decorated a rented trailer with streamers and balloons. And, of course, we also had photo buttons of our children to wear. The football team rode in the back of the trailer for a grand total of five minutes. We then tore off the streamers and balloons, because the trailer had to be returned. After the game, we had a feast and a party.

I felt sick. *Look at all we have. Look at the waste. Look at how over the top it is.* The little boy with half of a T-shirt and his soccer balls made of plastic bags continued to flash in my mind. The contrast between our two situations was vast. I had to do something. I emailed our mission partner and told her that I would like to buy soccer balls for the kids in Malawi. Could she buy them there? Would it be helpful, or would it just be more work for her?

She responded by telling me of an upcoming youth camp. One hundred different churches would each be sending two children to attend. In addition to balls, they would love to have T-shirts and Bibles to give to each child who attended. The balls would be used by the youth clubs to prepare for the annual "Msungamoyo [Preserve Life] Trophy" sponsored by World Relief Malawi.

I got to work. I was given the name of a generous family in Chicago who loved soccer. With one phone call to them, I was able to get fifty soccer balls donated, and money was given to cover the cost of fifty netballs—the favored game of Malawian girls. With more emails and phone calls, T-shirts were donated at cost, and money for the Bibles was donated. I couldn't have planned all of this by myself. I sensed that God was on the move.

A week or so later, I showed the picture of the Malawian boy in his ragged shirt to a friend. She handed back the photo, and as I stared at this African boy, the face of a little American boy came to my mind. Continents and decades apart, but they looked like they could have been brothers. The American face that came to my mind was that of a little boy I played with every day after school on the farm. We played dodgeball and danced together outside his two-room concrete block home. His home was in the shadow of my large, five-bedroom, two-story home sitting on 150 acres of farmland. His father worked in the tobacco and cotton fields of our farm, and his mother worked in our home, cleaning, cooking, and caring for our family. This little boy was my best friend growing up.

I realized that God's upper story and my lower story had just collided. The upper story of God's work of restoration in the world, meeting the needs of kids in Africa, and my lower story, growing up on a farm as a child, had just collided. God can use all of our stories for His purposes. God wants us to have the thrill of doing his work of bringing heaven to earth. This was the little slice of heaven that I felt He was calling me to bring down to earth.

As I worked on acquiring balls, Bibles, and T-shirts for the kids in Malawi, my heart kept turning to thoughts of Africa. For most of my life, I have repeatedly prayed under my breath the following: "God, please don't send me to Africa." This is not likely something that most people think about. However, my great-aunt Neale (as you may recall, our daughter shares her first name, and Neale is my middle name) was a missionary in Nigeria for forty-two years. As her namesake, I heard all about the amazing work she did with the young woman there, but I also heard her stories of snakes, of being away from home for three-year stints, and of her brush with death when she contracted blackwater fever, so I feared following in her footsteps.

Breathless Haste

Jay and I continued to sense that our season at the church in Chicago was drawing to a close. Our six-year stint there had been amazing, but

Breathless Haste

our souls were restless. Jay was in a job that was killing him inside; his greatest abilities were no longer being called on, and his passion for this church's

> **"He brought us to Chicago—our first walk on the water. Now He's asking us to get out of the Chicago boat and walk on the water to something else."**
>
> **May 2009**

work was gone. He was just punching a time clock, and it was very hard to watch.

In April 2009, I met with my spiritual director, a person who comes alongside another to listen for God's activity. I told her how tired I was of being asked where I was from. Apparently my Southern accent had not faded a bit, and it was constant evidence that I was far from home. Each time I was asked, I wanted to scream that I was from the South and I didn't really want to live in the Midwest and forever shovel snow. But instead, most of the time, I just bit my tongue and kindly said, "South Carolina."

I also discussed with her the unease that we were feeling. She said that the God of Israel who had summoned us by name would summon us again in the fullness of time. The revelation awaited an appointed time. She then reached behind her chair to grab a Bible from a basket of books. She opened it up to Habakkuk 2:1–4 and read this to me: "At the destined hour it will come in breathless haste, it will not fail. If it delays, wait for it; for when it comes will be no time to linger."

I said to her, "Breathless haste? That's how we came to Chicago, basically swept up and carried away in an instant. I wonder if that's how we will leave?" I went home and began to look through every translation of every Bible we had in our home. I couldn't find one version that even came close to the wording of "breathless haste." I went online and

Chapter Eight

searched and again found nothing. I finally asked her what version of the Bible she was using that day, and she said it was the New English Bible translation. Why did she grab such a nontraditional version of the Bible? Likely because those were the exact words I needed to hear at this particular moment in time.

Jay and I decided to do a thirty-day challenge with the Habakkuk 2 scripture she had read to me. We both were going to read it each day and then discuss what we were hearing or learning from it. It was a bit of a random idea. We had never done anything like that, nor have we since. One day I read it and then read the side notes in the Bible. It said that Habakkuk was on the watchtower with an attitude of expectation rather than fear; he wanted to be in the best position to hear God's Word.

During a solitude day, I was walking on the beautiful trails overlooking our Algonquin Lakes neighborhood that God had called us to six years earlier, and I heard a still, small voice say, "You

"I'm not fearful of a move. Staring over doesn't scare me now. I've seen what God can do if I let go of me and hang on to Him."

May 15, 2009

DON'T NEED TO KNOW WHERE YOU ARE CALLED TO NEXT. YOU JUST NEED TO KEEP DOING WHAT I AM ASKING YOU TO DO." I was all but sobbing.

Another day, I read and reread the Habakkuk scripture, and I noted, "I will stand. . . . I will take up my position." Habakkuk acted, and he prepared while he waited for the vision. The scripture also says, "Write down the vision." Jay and I decided it was time for him to write a résumé so that it was "ready to [be carried] with speed." Jay needed to actively participate in the process.

Jay and I unintentionally began taking turns on the watchtower at night. It just felt as if God nudged one of us awake frequently during that time. One night, he would be up at 3:00 or 4:00 a.m., and then another night, I would wake up. One day, I read the scripture again, and I noticed that it talked about *when* the vision comes, not *if*. Okay, God has a plan. Hang in there.

In addition to the Habakkuk text, I also read from other spiritual books. I opened *Strengthening the Soul of Your Leadership* by Ruth Haley Barton[19] early one morning. The sun peered over my shoulder and onto the page. I had a flashback to the morning that the light appeared on the words as I read in the chapel in South Carolina as God prepared my heart for the possible move to Illinois. It was a great reminder that if I am obedient to God's call on my life, then He will handle all the details. The words in Barton's book said, "The discernment process involves a major commitment to listening with love and attention . . . to those who will be affected most deeply by our decisions."[20] In my spirit, I heard that we needed to talk to our children about what was happening inside our souls. Since they were young, it had never occurred to me to include them in this decision-making process.

Soon after, Jay and I came together, and we told our thirteen-year-old daughter and our ten-year-old son that we felt that God was up to something. They asked if we were moving. Were we changing churches? We said that we didn't know any details—not when, not where. They responded with good questions rather than with anger, sadness, or concern. Neale said, "Dad, we can move if it will make you happy."

The conversation was holy ground, a time and place forever marked, a place where we experienced God with them right where we were, on that brown wrap-around corduroy couch in our den.

---

19 Ruth Haley Barton, *Strengthening the Soul of Your Leadership: Seeking God in the Crucible of Your Ministry* (Downers Grove, IL: IVP, 2018).
20 Barton, *Strengthening the Soul of Your Leadership*, 203.

Chapter Eight

Oddly enough, I began to envision a trapeze artist, one who has to let go of one bar before he can catch the next. It felt as if God was asking us to be in that place of letting go of the church in Chicago before the next bar was in sight. Frightening for sure. On one of my nights on the watchtower, I was reading John Ortberg's book *If You Are Going to Walk on Water, You Have to Get Out of the Boat*. And there, I read a story about a trapeze artist (182).[21] Confirmation again.

My parents came to visit, and I told them of our search for what was next for our family. My father said, "Well I'd like to tell you what to do, but I will yield to the Lord." The man who more than anything wanted us to move back and take over the family farm had just given us permission to pursue God's plans once again.

My mother shared these words from a devotional: "A mind that is alive to every word from God gives a constant opportunity for his divine interference with a suggestion that may alter the course of their lives by the faintest breath of feeling or the lightest touch of thought. We must always be on alert for His divine interference, because He knows what is best for us and for the world." Having our children and parents involved in the process was a gift. Even though we were all open to God's plans for us, I think beneath the surface we were all sending rallying cries to God, praying to have Him bring us back home.

A Scrapbook

Our mission partner was back in Chicago for another visit and was working with Jay on the plans for the next mission trip to Malawi. We took her out for her favorite dinner of Chinese food. The best Chinese restaurant ever happened to be directly across the street from our neighborhood. As we savored egg rolls and the beef and broccoli dish,

---

21 Ortberg, *Walk on Water*, 182.

Breathless Haste

I told her I was considering being a part of the next trip. Jay asked her how she might want me to serve.

She asked, "Do you like arts and crafts? . . . Would you be interested in helping AIDS families make scrapbooks?" She described how the children are left with nothing once their parents die. They have no pictures to keep and nothing to hold on to.

I almost fell out of my chair. What she didn't know was that I have been scrapbooking since I was seven years old. It is part of who I am and what I love to do—capturing the stories and milestones of life in a book. I had never dreamed that it could serve a larger purpose. That gave me the courage to sign up to be a part of the Malawi mission team in the summer of 2009, led by none other than my favorite, Jay.

As we prepared for the trip, we had a strong sense that it would somehow mark the finish line for us. We took a flight from Chicago to Atlanta, then the fifteen-hour flight to Johannesburg, South Africa, and we then spent the night there to let our bodies catch up with our souls, or vice versa. The next flight was three hours to Malawi. When our mission team arrived in Lilongwe, some of our luggage was missing. We continued on without it, since we had to get going on the ten-hour drive to Chitipa. We weren't sure that our luggage would ever be seen again.

All along the route, we saw clay mud huts, straw roofs, and women walking on the sides of the roads as they balanced either large water buckets or bundles of six-foot limbs of firewood on their heads. When we stopped for the night, I told Jay I needed to go home. My heart and mind couldn't take in or process what I was seeing for the first time. It felt to me like a movie set rather than reality. But leaving was not an option at this point. After a little bit of sleep under a mosquito net, I managed to get up the nerve to continue on, sitting in a nice seat in a small bus with air conditioning, quickly making our way up the road, which was sometimes paved and sometimes not.

Once we settled at our destination, my first assignment was to visit the home of a family with HIV/AIDS. I was thousands of miles away from my beautiful two-story, four-bedroom home in Chicago. The family, a friend from church, and I sat on a large straw mat outside of the one-room, red, mud-brick home. The husband and wife both had HIV/AIDS, and they had a six-week-old baby girl. Gut-wrenching.

We were there to encourage them, pray for them, and deliver gifts of sugar, oil, and soap, and we were asked to take pictures of us giving the gifts to the family. It felt like a photo-op. White, rich girl gives to the poor. I didn't want a picture that portrayed me as some sort of heroine in this situation. I was overwhelmed and uncomfortable with the poverty, sickness, and sadness of all that I had witnessed. I wanted to run back to the comforts of my home, far away from all of this. And I certainly didn't need a photograph of the scene, as it will always be seared into my memory.

The next day, we were scheduled to help families make memory books. As we arrived at the very old, one-room brick community center, our team stepped off the bus to the sight and sound of the participants clapping and singing with great joy over us. It was the closest I've ever felt to being a celebrity. It was a lot to take in.

We began to unpack the luggage with all the scrapbooks, scissors, and paper. I had collected so many Creative Memories supplies from friends and neighbors that it was actually embarrassing. I wasn't aware until I arrived that most of the people I was here to serve have only rare access to a pen or a piece of paper. I had brought too much stuff.

Breathless Haste

We brought instant cameras and film to take pictures of the families. The family photo would develop right before their eyes. We also provided questions for them to answer so they could capture their family histories, traditions, and desires. I learned that these books would also help by serving as a will of sorts, that would help these people to preserve their land and homes after death.

On the first day, we had about twenty families show up to create their books. One of the women who walked through the door was none other than the woman with the six-week-old baby I had visited the day before. I had no idea that I would ever see her again. We greeted and hugged each other.

Our group asked the families to scatter around the room at small wooden tables. The Malawian leaders helped them to answer the questions about their histories, while our team took photos, showed them samples, and demonstrated how to use the papers, colored pens, and stickers to decorate their books. Each family made good progress with their scrapbooks. We told them to return the next day with any other family members they would like to have pictures taken of, or to bring any photos from home they wanted to include in the books.

The next day, in God's perfect timing, my lost luggage arrived with the rest of the scrapbook supplies, including alphabet stickers. The participants were excited to see them, and they all wanted to use the stickers to put their names in their books. At one point, I walked over to the woman with the six-week-old baby, and in her scrapbook, she was spelling out her name: R-A-B-E-C-C-A. How many women in Africa have that name? I can't imagine very many. I felt as if God was saying to me, "I KNOW THAT YOU ARE OVERWHELMED WITH ALL YOU HAVE SEEN, BUT I AM ASKING YOU TO BRING HOPE TO ONE PERSON AT A TIME, AND I AM CONFIRMING

Chapter Eight

THAT BY CONNECTING YOU WITH SOMEONE ELSE WHO HAS YOUR NAME." I don't think Rabecca will forget me, and I certainly will not forget her.

As we walked out of the building that day, we noticed the village children had taken the sticker remnants from the trash and had adorned their bodies. They had stickers everywhere, and they were grinning from ear to ear. So were we.

In addition to scrapbooking, the mission team helped to host a soccer camp for the children as well as a Bible training conference for pastors from around Chitipa. It was a life-changing trip for me. Seeing the primitive homes, the poverty, and the lack of water and electricity in this century was heartbreaking, but meeting the people and seeing their great joy and deep faith was inspiring. There is a very thin space between God and them, as they have to pray constantly for the next meal, for rain, and for surviving to the next day. We, on the other hand, have so much that stands between God and us: money, possessions, busyness, and work, all of which are barriers to deeper faith and prayer.

When we returned home from this trip, we reunited with our children. We looked to the horizon, to the right, and to the left to see if there were any sightings of the finish line. There was nothing apparent, so we resumed our positions on the watchtower.

FOR REFLECTION

Take a few minutes to journal in response to these questions:

- ▶ What photo causes you to have a flashback to your past? When have you sensed God using your past to help someone in the here and now?
- ▶ Have you ever been struck by the vast needs in the world and felt compelled to do something about it? What was that experience like for you?
- ▶ Where have you seen God's upper story (the work of restoration in the world) collide with your own lower story?
- ▶ How might God use a passion, gift, or hobby you enjoy for a greater good in our world?

CHAPTER NINE

A Poem, a Phone Call, and a Baby Bonnet
(Jay)

> Trust in the LORD and do good; dwell in the land and enjoy safe pasture. Take delight in the LORD, and he will give you the desires of your heart.
> —PSALM 37:3-4

The time between having my heart broken in Africa and returning a year later with Rebecca was very difficult. My frustrations with the organizational culture at the megachurch continued to mount. One of the reasons I went there was for the vision of changing lives through the local church. I had been there for more than six years, and it seemed that the cost was now greater than the vision. I could feel the frustration turning to bitterness. One of my favorite writings from Dietrich Bonhoeffer is his poem "Who Am I,"[22] which he wrote from prison. In it, he said that he was "weary and empty in prayer, in thinking, in doing, / weak, and ready to take leave of it all." That is exactly how I felt.

---

22 Geoffrey B. Kelly and F. Burton Nelson. *A Testament to Freedom: The Essential Writings of Dietrich Bonhoeffer*. (New York: Harper Collins, 1990, 1995), 539.

One cold winter morning, I arrived early at work and tried to unlock my office door. After several failed attempts, I suddenly realized that I was trying to unlock it with the electronic fob for my car. Clearly, something needed to change. For the past year, I had been praying the same prayer, "Restore my passion for this church and put me in a role that fits me, or release me." However, nothing changed. If anything, it got worse, with more reorganizations, more chaos, and more devaluing experiences for friends, staff, and for me. More of all the wrong things.

The one area where I still felt passion was in the church's global efforts. I was serving on their Africa board and loved what they were doing outside the walls of the church. I also trusted those leading these global efforts. I was encouraged by Warren, the staff member who led the global ministry, to consider leaving my area pastor role and pursue a role with his team. Warren was someone I respected, and I was excited by the possibility of being mentored by him. He had transitioned to ministry from the world of finance, and I related to how God had used his business background to make the world a better place. He told me that he and John, the leader of their work in Africa, had said that if they ever were to go down in a plane, I was someone who could take their place. It felt good to be valued, and the new opportunity sounded like a perfect fit.

I felt that this would be a great opportunity to move on from neighborhood ministry and work in a functional, life-giving environment with someone I trusted. So I interviewed with the person who led the compassion and justice effort. I was excited about the possibility, believing this role would restore my passion for the church. It seemed like a great answer to my situation, and I had several people tell me that it made so much sense. I felt as if God was leading in that

Chapter Nine

direction. However, after a few weeks, someone from outside the church was chosen for the role. At the time, I was extremely disappointed. In hindsight, it was a huge blessing. Sometimes God closes a door to make room for another one to open.

During all of this, the ministry continued to churn unabated. In early April, I received a call about a terrible auto accident in my area. A young mom and her eight-year-old and six-year-old little girls had been in a head-on collision. The mom and eight-year-old were killed immediately, while the six-year-old hung on for ten days. I was in the middle of it with the family throughout that time, and I did the funeral for all three. Three coffins in the chapel. Two of them were way too small. It was a gut-wrenching experience that brought back some of the worst times in my own life. That's a curious thing about ministry: the things your story has most equipped you for are sometimes the most painful. Just before the service, Rebecca walked into my office. She was there to attend the funeral to support me. It was an act of sacrificial love; she was willing to enter a painful situation that would bring back so many terrible memories for her. It was the kind of situation I would have avoided if possible. Even after all we had been through, we still approached grief and tragedy in our own ways, but always together.

It was during this time that we had been given the Habakkuk scripture. I was standing in the watchtower, journaling, praying, exhausted from waiting, and still with no clue what to do next. I sensed that God had released me from the church in Chicago. That I was free to go. In the past few years, I had heard a number of people use that term: released. It seemed strange when I first heard it, but now it made sense. My time was done, but when would I leave, and where would I go next? As I read the words from Habakkuk that said, "Write down the vision,

Breathless Haste

inscribe it on tablets, ready for a herald to carry it," I felt prompted to write my resignation letter. Sometimes it's helpful to write out your feelings as a way of processing them, so that is what I did. I wrote in my journal what I wanted to say when I resigned. Seeing it on paper felt like a step toward moving on.

On May 14, 2009, at 3:30 a.m., I was awake, writing in my journal, wondering why God would not speak. For more than a year, I had asked for a new calling at the church where I served or somewhere else. Why was He not speaking? Then I had a thought: *What if He was speaking through His silence?* Maybe God was asking me to leave this job first, and then He would tell me where to go. The Habakkuk verse said, "I will watch to learn what [God] will say through me, and what shall I reply . . . the LORD [will] answer" (NEB, emphasis added). Maybe that is why I had written the resignation letter. What if, as with Abraham, God was asking me to leave before he told me where to go? (Gen. 12:1). As I sat in my den in the middle of the night while my family was sleeping upstairs, I felt God leading me to just walk away.

The next morning, I shared all of this with Rebecca, which I am pretty sure ruined her day. Rebecca was not getting paid for her ministry work, we had two children and a mortgage, and this was 2009, when the economy was terrible. I had a significant role at one of the most influential churches in America, and yet I thought God was telling me to walk away from it and see what happened. If we did this, it would indeed prove to be God's word for me or the dumbest decision I had ever made.

When a pastor is struggling with the organizational culture of their church, it can be such an isolating experience. In whom can you confide? It's not appropriate or safe to talk with people in the congregation. How

Chapter Nine

could you share with someone who found Jesus there, someone who loves the church, the sermons, and the music, that the reality on the inside is different from the outside, and that the staff is struggling. I decided to get advice from a couple of pastors I trusted who had left the church. I also had a conversation about a role with another church nearby. I wasn't sure about the fit, but Rebecca's mentor, Sibyl, said, "He needs to hear himself say what he wants to do." However, in my heart, my desire was to go home if I left the church in Chicago. This idea of quitting was scary, but in a strange way it also felt freeing.

I was leading the upcoming trip to Malawi in late June, and Rebecca was going with me. She convinced me that I should put this idea of walking away from my job on pause until after the trip. Since I was leading the trip to a place that I loved with a team I loved, it was an easy sell. We continued to think, pray, and get advice from a small group of people we trusted. As with other times when I thought I heard God's voice, confirming it through spiritually mature people was crucial.

One of those people was Reggie McNeal. A few years earlier, I emailed Reggie after reading his book *The Present Future*.[23] The book made clear that we really needed to rethink some of our paradigms for the church. We connected because we both lived in the tension of being frustrated by the church and loving the church at the same time. I told him that I could not believe he wrote that book and worked for the South Carolina Baptist Convention. He responded that he couldn't believe that I liked the book and worked where I did! Later, I attended an event with him, and we began a friendship. When I called Reggie to talk to him about how I thought God was leading me, I asked if he thought I was

---

23 Reggie McNeal, *The Present Future: Six Tough Questions for the Church* (San Francisco, CA: Jossey-Bass, 2003).

hearing from God, losing my mind, or both. That's when he asked me a question that would change the trajectory of my family's life.

He asked, "Have you ever heard of Peachtree Presbyterian Church in Atlanta?" I said I didn't know much about it other than the fact that it was a large Presbyterian church. He said he had just led a conference for them and thought he should introduce me to Vic, the senior pastor. So, on June 3, he introduced us via email. Within a day or so, Vic asked me to send him my résumé. Because of Peachtree's size, I wasn't expecting such a quick response. I looked at some things about missional church on their website and told Rebecca that it sounded as if I had written it. And that was it, just another seemingly random networking connection.

A Poem

At the same time I was investigating the Peachtree position, the possibility of another global role at the church resurfaced. I was willing to explore it, but I sensed that God had released me, and it was time to move on. I don't read a lot of poetry, but for some reason, during this time several poems resonated with me. Steve, a close spiritual friend from our neighborhood who knew about my sense that we were moving toward a transition, suggested a poem titled "The Journey," by Mary Oliver.[24] It was such an accurate portrayal of my feelings.

> It was already late
> enough, and a wild night,
> and the road full of fallen
> branches and stones.

---

24 Mary Oliver, "The Journey," *No Voyage and Other Poems* (Boston: Houghton Mifflin, 1965).

Chapter Nine

I felt that it was already late enough. So much had happened in these past couple of years at the church that could not be unseen or unfelt. I really needed to move on to a place where I could once again lead out of my authentic self. I read that poem over and over and even wrote it out in my journal several times. It put words to my emotions about my own journey and sense that it was time, in the poet's words, to "save / the only life that I could / save."

Let me be clear. Poetry is not the Word of God as Scripture is. However, I do think God can use poetry, music, or snow in the crook of a tree to guide us along the way. Anything can be used by the Spirit. "The wind blows wherever it pleases" (John 3:8). When we resonate with something on a deep level, we must wonder why and determine if it's connected with a God-given desire. It was becoming clear that when my desire and God's desire aligned, it would be time for me to move on.

In late June, Rebecca and I left for the trip to Malawi. It was the only thing remaining that I was passionate about doing. In fact, it had been a welcome diversion from the stress of discerning my next steps.

> **"I am seriously considering resigning after I return from Africa—just letting go and trusting that God will show us what is next."**
>
> **May 14, 2009**

As Rebecca mentioned earlier, it was her first trip, and it was a time for her to see what I had seen and feel what I had felt. It included a canceled flight, lost luggage, terrible roads, and several breakdowns with a vehicle that was a part of the "convenient car hire" company. Despite all that, God did some amazing things in us and through us. It was a powerful experience for the whole team.

The team spent the last couple of days at an inn on Lake Malawi. It was a time to relax before returning home. Rebecca and I sat on the beach and talked about the trip and what lay ahead upon our return. That week in Malawi had filled our minds and hearts. It had been a time that drew us closer together through the sharing of difficult experiences. It had been a break from trying to find our next steps. As always for us, it was good to have a beach nearby when we were facing a crucial life decision.

Rebecca had encouraged me not to make any decisions about leaving my position at the church until after this trip to Malawi. Now as we sat beside the water and talked, watching the fishermen in their dugout canoes, I could feel the anxiety returning, that feeling in the pit of my stomach I had knowing that, when we returned, we had to go back to the tension of making a major life decision. The morning we left the lake, I sat on some rocks at the edge of the water and watched the sun rise. The words of Psalm 23 ran through my mind: "He leads me by still waters. He restores my soul" (ESV). It now felt like time to go back and make a final decision and trust that God would lead me to "green pastures."

A Phone Call

We arrived back in Chicago on a Wednesday afternoon. I went into the office the following day, Thursday, July 2. We were approaching a holiday weekend, and I wanted to catch up on my emails after being away. I had been in my office for a couple of hours when I received a phone call. The caller introduced herself as Marnie, the executive pastor at Peachtree Presbyterian Church in Atlanta. She said that she and Vic had been talking and wondered if I would be interested in exploring a role with them. I told her that we were coming to South Carolina for vacation the first week of August and asked her if that would work for their schedule. She said they really wanted me to come down in the next

Chapter Nine

couple of weeks, because Vic was in town during his summer break. I explained that I would have to figure out how to be away from work since I had just returned, but that I would look at my schedule and be in touch soon.

The timing was uncanny. I walked outside to call Rebecca. When I told her what had happened, she started crying. After a year of praying and being on the verge of leaping off the cliff without a landing spot, this felt as if it really might be it. I had never seen the church or met the people, but it was hard to ignore His timing. Through the years, I have learned that God's timing is perfect, and it is rarely early. After all the waiting and wondering, and now the first day back from Africa I received this call about an interview that had to happen quickly. It seemed like something akin to breathless haste—again.

> **"It does feel like God—especially the timing."**
> *July 3, 2009*

With so much happening so quickly, it seemed that the dam had burst. In the two weeks before going to Atlanta, I had another discussion about a global role at the church and conversations with another church in Chicago and one in Charlotte. My head was spinning. I also reached out to some friends from the Presbyterian world to do some due diligence on Peachtree. In all honesty, I was jaded at this point and wanted to make sure I was not moving to another church mess—one with a Southern accent this time. I even talked with someone who had left Peachtree under negative circumstances. I had no question that God was guiding us, but at the same time, I believe He gives us a mind to think and reason along with Him. Hearing God's voice isn't a passive process, but an interactive participation with the work of the Spirit.

Breathless Haste

Twelve days after landing in a plane inbound from Malawi, I was outbound on another flight to Atlanta. I spent a couple of days at Peachtree, meeting with Vic and the other pastors on staff. It was a great visit and felt very comfortable, like putting on that old favorite sweater. In some ways, it was a surprise, because after more than six years at a nondenominational church, I had not thought I would ever be back in a more traditional church. However, Peachtree felt like a place where my worlds might converge. I understood the Presbyterian context, felt theological compatibility, and could still have space to innovate. We decided that our family would return in three weeks on August 7—Brock's birthday, of all days—for a follow-up visit.

While the speed of this potential opportunity was increasing, I was also holding back, trying to keep an open hand in case God said no. I was also probably guarding my heart, remembering my disappointment with the global position a year earlier. In addition, the timing created a challenge for my integrity and my commitment to follow God's voice. I believed that from that April when I awakened at 3:00 a.m., God was asking me to walk away from the church in Chicago before having another job. Now it seemed that he had shown me a path forward. The trouble was that my annual review with my manager was scheduled for August 4, three days before my return to Atlanta for my second interview.

The annual review was a time to talk about the past year and what I was planning for the year ahead. How could I do that? How could I talk about my plans for the year ahead knowing that I was leaving one way or another? I talked with a few close colleagues at church, and they all advised me not to let management know that I was in process with another church. They said if I did that, I would be done. Of course, in my heart, I was already done. If I believed that God told me to leave without another job, how could I now, with the Peachtree opportunity on the horizon, backtrack and play it safe?

I went ahead and met with my manager and told her the truth, that I was in an interview process with another church, and it seemed likely it would happen soon. She seemed surprised but gracious, and I left feeling that I had done the right thing. I wanted to leave, but I also wanted to leave well. Despite my frustrations, I loved the people in my area and did not want to leave them in a bad position. Three days later we were in Atlanta as a family to explore this opportunity. Our kids were a part of this process, and we wanted them to feel good about whatever we did. This move could change the trajectory of their lives as well. We were so thankful that we had brought them into our process months earlier in Chicago.

A Baby Bonnet

On Saturday morning, Rebecca and I had breakfast with Vic. He shared the story of how the Peachtree church began. In 1909, a couple in a horse and buggy were on their way home from the funeral of their four-month-old son, Lance. They noticed children playing along the road and decided to start a Sunday school for those children to honor the memory of their son. The church grew from there, and Lance's baby bonnet is contained in the cornerstone of the church. As Vic shared this story, Rebecca and I looked at each other, knowing what the other was thinking. The convergence of their story and ours was amazing. If we had a cornerstone for our life in ministry, it would contain something from Brock's life. Here we were, one hundred years later in a restaurant located on the property near where their home once stood, feeling led to be a part of carrying on their vision.

Breathless Haste

I was offered the position of pastor for mission later that day. I told them I needed to talk it over with our children. We had told them that they would be part of our decision, and we needed to honor that. A couple of days later we were at the beach house in South Carolina for the annual family gathering, and the children were in the pool. I said, "So what do y'all think?" They smiled and gave a big thumbs-up. Later, Neale helped me press send on the resignation email to my boss in Chicago that I had composed months earlier. That day was also the first day of school in Atlanta. We had no idea where we would live or what schools they would attend, so more frenetic weeks ensued.

The last verses from the Habakkuk passage say that the reckless will be unsure of themselves, but the righteous will live by being faithful. We were sure because of our faith, and we knew that following God wasn't reckless. So, *"I see so clearly how God has been moving in my life over these years to get me to this part of the journey." July 16, 2009* with breathless haste, we put a "for sale" sign in the yard of our house in Chicago, packed our personal belongings in that same old Honda minivan, and drove our family of four, plus our dog, back to the South to live in the basement of Rebecca's sister, who lived just two miles from Peachtree. It was only four months after we intently sought God's will for our family using the verses from Habakkuk.

I went back to Chicago for the transition, to say goodbye to friends, and to embrace a flood of memories. I had an Africa board meeting in the same room where Rebecca wept on the carpet on our first visit six years earlier. Finally, on my last Sunday after the services, I walked into the empty, recently-built 7,200-seat church auditorium—a space where so many had heard God's voice—for one last look. As I stood there,

"Resurrection" by Nicol Sponberg[25] began to play over the speakers. The words spoke to the condition of my soul. I, too, could no longer fake it. I was desperately in need of resurrection.

In retrospect, I could see the perfection of God's timing. I had thought that I was ready to leave in 2008. If that had happened, I would have left angry. Now, a year later, after many prayers, conversations, and words written in my journal, I was prepared to turn the page in a healthy way. I was leaving in a good place, sad about the things that I couldn't change but forever grateful for the amazing gift of my time there. God had transformed my life and ministry through the people I had served with in that place. I had gained a more holistic view of the gospel, reconciled difficult parts of my own story, had my heart opened for the poor, and had seen how God worked in and through the broken parts of the church. In the end, the Monet painting finally seemed to be in proper focus.

FOR REFLECTION

Take a few minutes to journal in response to these questions:

- ▶ When have you hoped and prayed for something, only to be disappointed? In retrospect, can you see how God might have closed a door to open another one?
- ▶ Describe an experience where the timing seemed uncanny. Is there a season in your own life where you can relate to Jay's statement, "I have learned that God's timing is perfect, and it is rarely early"?
- ▶ Have you ever felt led to make a decision that seemed illogical? If so, how do you distinguish between a prompting and a crazy idea?

---

25 Nicol Sponberg, "Resurrection," *Resurrection* (Curb Record, 2007).

CHAPTER TEN

A Neighbor, Dallas Willard, and Bankruptcy (Rebecca)

> This is what the LORD says: "Stand at the crossroads and look; ask for the ancient paths, ask where the good way is, and walk in it, and you will find rest for your souls.
>
> —JEREMIAH 6:16

A Neighbor

Jennifer, a neighbor in Algonquin Lakes who became a dear soul friend, participated in my Listen to My Life neighborhood group. During that process, she felt led to enter into the spiritual direction program at North Park Seminary. She convinced me to look into the program as well. It was about listening to God, listening to God with another, and listening to God in community. It lined up perfectly with my ministry work, so I applied, was accepted, and began my work in the program in the summer of 2009. At the same time, I was also working on packing, sorting, and cleaning out the house in preparation for the potential move to Atlanta. When I attended the first session on the North Park campus in Chicago, it felt as if this was the preparation of my heart and soul for the next leg of our journey.

When I returned from the class, the move to Atlanta was a go. I was delighted that I would be back in the South and within driving distance of my family, my family's farm, and the homeplace of my great-grandparents, grandparents, and parents. One of the bedrooms there claimed the honor of being the birthplace of my father in 1920. As my father and his three brothers grew up, my grandparents were very successful with cotton crops and the development of a high-yielding cotton seed. As the boll weevil devastated cotton fields throughout the South, my grandparents turned their attention to dairy farming. They were devoted to the farm, family, God, and Ebenezer Baptist Church, which was just a couple of miles away from their home. My parents continued that tradition of devotion to their faith and the same church. My father expanded the farm operation with tobacco, soybean, corn, and wheat crops, and he added real estate and hotel developments to his holdings. He was always working on the next big deal, and he was always able to borrow more and more money to put the deals together. Our family joked that he was playing a real-life Monopoly game. For his eightieth birthday, the Monopoly theme was integrated into the celebration; it showed up in the cake, plates, hats, and poems. As a gift, we even had a custom-made Monopoly game created with all my father's businesses. I am the lucky one who has possession of it now.

As the economy went into a deep recession in 2009, we made our move back to the South, and my family's businesses and holdings began to unravel. For estate planning purposes, years earlier, most of my father's estate was put into his four daughters' names, including mine.

Chapter Ten

Along the way, we had signed many loans to keep it all going. Yes, I was naïve, but it was what my sisters and I did to keep all of it afloat. After all, it always seemed to work out. On paper, the assets were always far greater than the liabilities. However, this time, as the economy slowed to a halt, the banks began to call the loans, and there was not enough money to pay the debts that had been racked up. We had millions of dollars in debt when all the beans were counted.

We were struggling financially at a personal level too, as our home in Chicago was hard to offload in the recessional market. We were paying a large mortgage in Chicago and hefty rent on our home in Atlanta for months on end. It was a very financially stressful time, especially for me, as I had often struggled with my relationship with money.

Early in 2011, Peachtree Church offered Dave Ramsey's Financial Peace class, so I asked Jay to take it with me. In one of the videos we watched, I heard an accountant say that he was going to deliver pizza as a second job in order to get out of debt, and I felt a strong impression in my spirit that I wasn't above delivering pizza. While the ministry work with Listen to My Life was very fulfilling and purposeful, it wasn't bringing in income for our family.

Before we completed the class, I asked Jay, "What is your takeaway from the class?"

Jay said, "You need to get a job."

I didn't like that idea, because I loved the one I had. However, I realized with our children going to college in a few years, a money-making job would be a huge help. I started looking at IT jobs, since my post-college career was with IBM.

A dear Peachtree friend called and asked if I knew that Peachtree was looking for a part-time person to work with Fuller Seminary. That piece of information opened up a work conversation with Peachtree's executive pastor, Marnie, the same person who had hired Jay two years earlier. The next thing I knew, I had started a part-time job helping Fuller Seminary to market, execute, and host seminary classes on Peachtree's campus. In addition, I connected with Peachtree visitors and taught membership classes with Marnie. God can even use thoughts of pizza delivery jobs to direct us down the right path.

When it was time for me to go back to Chicago for the second year of the North Park program, there were a dozen financial and scheduling reasons it didn't make sense for me to attend, so I sat that year out. When I found out the week I was to attend the following year, my heart sank. It was the same week I was to be in Florida for my daughter's national softball tournament. I couldn't miss that. I had only three more years with her before she would be off to college.

Dallas Willard

I began asking God if He was closing the door on the spiritual direction program. Should I give up finishing the degree? Was there something else for me? I watched, listened, and waited. As part of the North Park program, I was to have ongoing sessions with a spiritual director. A friend in the program recommended a director named Gary, who lived in Atlanta. In one of my meetings with him, I asked for his input about other spiritual direction programs.

He said, "Well, I am biased, but I think Renovaré is one of the best things out there..."

I'd never heard of it. He told me to read some of Richard Foster and Dallas Willard's books to see if I connected with them.

Chapter Ten

I then said, "I'll know in the first two chapters whether I connect with it or not." I have no idea why those words just spewed out of my mouth. Such an odd thing to say.

"Perhaps Renovaré? I probably should read a Dallas Willard book to see if I even like him!"

June 2010

I came home and previewed Richard Foster's *Celebration of Discipline*[26] online, and this is what it said in the first chapter of the book:

> We must not be led to believe that the disciplines are only for spiritual giants . . . or for those who are contemplatives who devote all their time to prayer and meditation. Far from it. God intends the disciplines of the spiritual life to be for ordinary human beings: people who have jobs, who care for children, who must wash dishes and mow lawns. In fact, the disciplines are best exercised in the midst of our normal daily activities. . . . in our relationships with our husband or wife, our brothers and sisters, our friends and neighbors.[27]

There have been many occasions when written words have deeply spoken to me. This was one of them. I was in tears one more time.

I was getting ready to leave on a trip to Costa Rica with some other church members, so I hurriedly sought a copy of that book to take with me. My church bookstore had one copy. I grabbed it. Next, I had an email from our senior pastor that included a quotation from Dallas Willard. Then, on Sunday, another pastor had a different Dallas Willard quotation up on the video screen.

---

26 Richard J. Foster, *Celebration of Discipline: The Path to Spiritual Growth* (San Francisco, CA: HarperOne, 2018)
27 Foster, *Discipline*, 1.

I went to my Sunday school class, and we began to talk about books we might want to read together. Someone said, "Richard Foster's *Celebration of Discipline* is a great book."

You have got to be kidding me. Really? Two Dallas Willard quotations and a Richard Foster book all mentioned within forty-eight hours.

We arrived in Costa Rica, and one of the church members told us that he was staying for an extra couple of days for some solitude and reading. I asked him what he brought to read. The first book he mentioned? *Celebration of Discipline*. Again, if this had happened once, I wouldn't have noticed, but when things like this happen repeatedly and almost concurrently, it's best to pay attention.

A week or so later, I was driving around Atlanta, and I suddenly wondered if I had wasted a year by going through spiritual direction at North Park. I then recounted the circumstances that led me to the Renovaré Institute: my neighbor Jennifer, who participated in Listen to My Life, encouraged me to enter the program at North Park, then a friend at North Park connected me to Gary, and then Gary connected me to Renovaré. As these thoughts were streaming through my head, the song "Walk Down this Mountain" by Bebo Norman[28] began playing in the car. Even though the words sung didn't directly address my situation, they just moved in my heart enough for me to know it was the final confirmation that Renovaré was my next step. Soon thereafter, I applied and was accepted to the cohort that was beginning in Atlanta, of all places.

This Renovaré spiritual formation program included instruction from some amazing teachers, including Dallas Willard, Jan Johnson,

---

28 Bebo Norman, "Walk Down this Mountain," *Ten Thousand Days* (Watershed Records, 1999).

Chapter Ten

James Bryan Smith, and others. I was in over my head at the deep end of the spiritual pool with these thoughtful, soulful, godly people. Through a deep dive into soul training and spiritual practices that included homework, reading, and lessons from these spiritual giants, I began to learn about living now in the kingdom of God.

In October 2011, I attended the first in-person residency week of the Renovaré program at the Monastery of the Holy Spirit in Conyers, Georgia. The monks of this monastery on the outskirts of Atlanta shared a portion of their beautiful 2,000-acre tract with walking trails, Holy Spirit Abbey Church, and a retreat center for our cohort to spend this time together.

The Renovaré leaders asked us to bring an object that represented our current life situation. As I was packing to go, I had an idea to grab my $2 bill as the object to share, not only as a representation of my desire for a better relationship with money, but also representing the financial mess I found myself in with my family.

As I turned off the exit to make my way to the monastery, I saw a homeless man on the side of the road. McDonald's was just across the street, so I headed there to buy him a gift card. As I ordered at the drive-through, they told me they had no gift cards. I ordered cookies for him, and then I felt a nudge to also put the $2 bill in the bag. It took me a few U-turns to get to him, but I finally pulled over and handed him the bag. He gave me a huge smile and responded with "God bless you."

Later that evening, I looked at the palm of my hand, where I had written "$2" in ink. It was my reminder not to forget to take the bill with me to the monastery. I shared with my Renovaré group about the financial and legal situation that was brewing beneath the surface for my family and me. We discussed how I might bring my family's real-life Monopoly game under the kingdom of God. I got the sense that I had already begun to take some baby steps toward that end—forgiving my father for the mess we were in, praying with my sister rather than praying apart, and giving the $2 bill to the homeless man.

During the week, we were invited into the Ignatian practice of experiencing Scripture. We were invited to use our senses, body, heart, and imagination to immerse ourselves in the scene and become a participant in the story as the scripture was read to us. In this practice, you try to envision yourself in a scene of Scripture. Mark 9:14–28 was the scripture selected. It is about the father who brought his son with epilepsy to Jesus to be healed. As I closed my eyes and listened to the scripture, tears began to form, and I felt as if I wanted to stretch out on the floor. I can't recall if I actually got down on the floor or not, but it felt like I had been transported to the scene. Immediately, I saw myself as the boy in the scene. He was foaming at the mouth and convulsing. In my thoughts, it was if I was foaming at the mouth and convulsing over my family's financial mess and being brought before Jesus for healing. It was the first time that I was personally "in" the scripture. It was very powerful. Slowly, we mentally and emotionally brought ourselves back to the room we were in, and we then discussed our Scripture experience with those around us.

The person next to me asked, "Have you thought of healing prayer for this?"

Healing prayers for finances and money? No, I had not. After Communion that night, I wrote in my journal, "God will do a healing work in your family." And then I wrote this prayer: "Guide us into Your way out."

Chapter Ten

As I previously mentioned, Dallas Willard was one of the teachers for Renovaré at the monastery that week. He was a best-selling author, reformer, Christian philosopher, and iconic Christian scholar. His primary teaching centered on how to live the eternal life now. Throughout the week, I noticed that others were meeting with him privately. I thought to myself, *He is brilliant, so what would I possibly have a conversation with him about?* But by the end of the week, I felt a prompting to meet with him. I requested a meeting, and he had one spot left. I took it. We met at a small table at the outdoor patio at the monastery. It was a gorgeous day. I was a bit nervous; it felt like a meeting with the Pope, but better.

I explained my family's massive financial mess that we were wallowing in. Dallas was very quiet for a long while, and then he said that we must get the best bankruptcy lawyer we could find. Not, *I'll be praying for you.* Not, *Let me pray for you now.* However, I believe that he prayed in that time of quiet before he responded, and I believe that was what God told him to tell me.

Bankruptcy

I walked back to the classroom after this bombshell piece of wisdom. It felt a bit surreal, but also very real at the same time. Our next class exercise was *Lectio Divina*, a repetitious, thoughtful meditation on Scripture. The instructor, Jan Johnson, read aloud the verses of 1 Corinthians 13:3-7: "If I give everything I own to the poor and even go to the stake to be burned as a martyr, but I don't love, I've gotten nowhere. So, no matter what I say, what I believe, and what I do, I'm bankrupt without love." (MSG)

Breathless Haste

Have you ever heard the term *bankrupt* in the Bible? Nor had I. And there is no way that Dallas Willard gave her the clue as we walked in the door. I am sure she had picked the scripture and prepared long before. According to these verses, the only way I am bankrupt in God's kingdom is if I am without love. I could be bankrupt according to the laws of South Carolina, but in God's kingdom, I am not bankrupt if I have love. I am a part of God's upside-down kingdom. That night, I participated in the healing service with my Renovaré cohort. When I walked up for prayer, I told the person that this would be the craziest topic for healing prayer that had ever been done.

He responded, "Bring it on."

I did, and so did he.

The next day, Psalm 23 was the scripture for our morning reflection. Out of forty students, I was asked to come up to sit in a chair. Jan Johnson anointed my head with oil as she read the scripture. It was so hard to take in what was happening at the moment. Later, I was told that an anointing is about a call, and a call is movement toward God. God was calling me to move toward Him in an area where my family had struggled.

I called my sister to discuss what Dallas told me. We both decided to ask around quietly for the best bankruptcy lawyer in South Carolina. We were trying to keep this family mess behind the scenes. When we compared our lists, the same name came up multiple times. This man had been working as a bankruptcy lawyer for more than thirty years in South Carolina. His ultimate goal for each case was to not file for bankruptcy—he preferred to shrewdly negotiate deals between the banks and companies outside of the courtroom. We hired him. During our time working with him, he would emphasize that each decision

Chapter Ten

was difficult, but in each situation, he would ask which solution was the "least bad thing."

Because my father was in his nineties, my sister and I were the ones to participate in the intense meetings with our bankruptcy lawyer, other lawyers, bankers, accountants, and real estate agents as we navigated this process. Almost daily, I was on the phone with someone, discussing something I was not qualified to understand, much less make a decision about. My repetitious prayer to God continued to be "Guide us into Your way out."

> **"I prayed . . . thank you for getting my grandparents through the depression, getting Daddy through World War II. Give us wisdom and courage to get through this."**
>
> *November 28, 2011*

This situation was stressful for Jay and me, as the ramifications of all the debt and legal proceedings could harm our nuclear family. We met with our own attorney; it was a hard discussion. As we left, Jay told me that I couldn't choose the best option for my extended family over what was best for our family. Tension was frequently in the air as we tried to navigate the financial unraveling that could also impact us personally.

Fast-forward a few months later, and I was back at my second Renovaré intensive, and I had to break away to talk with the bankruptcy lawyers. I sat in my car in the monastery parking lot, talking with them on the phone. Our lawyer told us that he hadn't been able to work out deals with all the parties involved, so we would have to file for bankruptcy. He asked us who would be signing the bankruptcy papers and who would do the depositions. I didn't want to do any of that. Perhaps my father would do it, but he was too old to handle this. To make matters worse, we were told in the same conversation that we were losing our beach house. The place where we had vacationed since I was a little girl. The place where we had shared countless conversations and meals seaside as extended family, and the place where we sought healing in Brock's death and wisdom for Neale's birth.

My heart was breaking. I was devastated on all fronts. I was so upset that I just left the monastery, drove an hour through Atlanta traffic, and went home for the evening. The next day, I reluctantly drove to Conyers and dragged myself back to the classroom. Richard Foster (yes, the author of *Celebration of Discipline*) offered up the opening prayer. In this prayer, he emphasized that God is with us in travail and that He sometimes smashes the idols we trust in.

We soon got the bankruptcy papers signed, and our lawyer went to court to file them. However, before he turned the papers over to the court, he had another case that day before a judge who was new to him. It must not have gone well. He told me that he thought if our case came before that judge, it could end up being an ugly mess for our family. Apparently, he felt so strongly about it that he decided not to file the papers. I believe that God intervened that day. Our lawyer instead went back to the table to negotiate with the parties involved, and he was able to work out deals with each one. I think him having the signed bankruptcy papers in hand gave him the last piece of leverage that he needed. Miraculously, we did not have to file bankruptcy.

We worked with lawyers, realtors, accountants, and banks for more than ten years before it was all behind us. All along the way, I prayed for God to bring whatever the deal or situation was under His kingdom. We ended up losing most of our family's holdings. Most of our assets were sold to pay off the banks, or they were simply turned over to the banks.

Chapter Ten

In the heartbreak of losing another of our beloved assets, the 150-acre family farm that sat right next to I-95, there was a beautiful ray of sunshine and hope. Instead of the farm being turned into an ugly commercial property and parking lot, the farm was sold to a local South Carolina foundation that wanted to develop it into a soccer complex for the Southeast. I told my friend Jennifer the story of the ending of the family farm. She wrote to me to say that she loved how children of many nations and tongues would be playing for generations to come on a land once segregated. The use of this land was once divided by race—there were the ones who owned the land and crops and the ones who worked the land and picked the crops. And now it would be filled with the laughter of all children playing together. That sounds like a kingdom-of-God, God's-beautiful-way-out kind of use of our farm, doesn't it?

In 2017, after most of the financial issues had been settled, my father died at ninety-six years of age. As we looked back on his life, it was like reading an amazing novel. He was a highly decorated World War II pilot, a United States congressman, and a real estate and agricultural entrepreneur. His absolute love and adoration of my mother extended for more than seventy years. Weekly, for more than fifty years, he taught a Sunday school class with my mother at our family's church, and he taught a Sunday school lesson broadcast live on the radio. He was, indeed, a devoted follower of Christ. I adored him, and he adored my three sisters, me, and our families. He was also beloved by his community and by many in the state of South Carolina. The flags in South Carolina were flown at half-mast the day of his funeral, evidence of his impact and the influence he had in the state where he had been born and lived his whole life.

Breathless Haste

We thought my mother might not withstand life without my father, but she continued to live for her daughters and grandchildren for several years. The last and most difficult piece of this family journey culminated when my mother passed away in 2021 at ninety-eight. She was the matriarch of our family. The markers of her life were her deep faith in God and her unconditional and unending love for each of her daughters, sons-in-law, and grandchildren. Her death triggered the movement of the final and most beloved asset in the Monopoly game: the homeplace of my family for almost 150 years was donated to the local foundation that had bought the surrounding farmland, as agreed to in the contract signed more than a decade earlier.

Cleaning out a home with that much history in a six-month window was overwhelming and another breathless-haste experience. Jay came alongside me each step of the way. It was one of his greatest gifts to me. We discovered deeds from the 1800s, my grandmother's wedding dress from the early 1900s, which we didn't know existed, and under a shelf in the attic, my parents' love letters, written during World War II and tied with a green ribbon in a Girl Scout cookie box. Along the way, I prayed that we would find all that needed to be found and that our family would not be in conflict as we divided the furnishings, family history, and treasures.

When my family came together in person and over Zoom to divide up what we had found, we began with a liturgy: "Sorting through a Loved One's Things" from *Every Moment Holy,* volume 2. "For by this service, we secure our bond even tighter. The depth of our love and the enduring significance of it all that we meant to another, remains.... Let us be reminded of your past faithfulness, present mercies and future hope."[29]

I believe that this family home and farm and the business successes surrounding it had become idols for my family and me. We were willing to incur rising amounts of debt to expand our portfolio with more hotels, more businesses, more land, and more houses. We risked it all and lost, but we kept what mattered—faith and love of family. Sometimes God asks us to tear down the idols, those we have constructed and/or those that have been handed down to us through the generations.

Even now, I am reminded of how easily I can make idols of the good things in my life that God has given me—family, purposeful work, home, productivity, abilities, income, and even this book. When I prioritize my relationship with Him first, then He will help me prioritize and gain the proper perspective on both the good gifts and the hard circumstances as they ebb and flow in my life.

The Monopoly game is now back in the box, and miraculously, my whole family is still gathering, still loving one another, and very much intact after a decade of dealing with this difficult mess. Every situation, no matter how big or small, can be brought underneath the kingdom of God as you listen, pray, and seek God's will. He can make a way out.

---

[29] Douglas Kaine McKelvey, "Sorting through a Loved One's Things," *Every Moment Holy, Volume II: Death, Grief, and Hope* (Nashville, TN: Rabbit Room, 2021), 276–277.

FOR REFLECTION

Take a few minutes to journal in response to these questions:

- ▶ When have you been encouraged to do something that would require you to stretch and grow? Did you follow through?
- ▶ Where might God be calling you to identify and tear down idols in your own life? Have any of these idols been passed down to you from your family?
- ▶ What difficult circumstances have you navigated? Who and what helped you get through it? Where have you seen evidence of God's presence with you?

EPILOGUE

Participation, Posture, and Preparation
(Jay)

Participation

In the tumultuous times in which we live, many wonder if God still works in people's ordinary lives at all—much less in extraordinary ways. Through our experiences of God's presence and His faithfulness to us, we know that He does. These experiences have taught us that life is an ongoing dynamic of God's grace and our response to it. We can't manipulate or find God through a prescribed formula, but neither can we sit passively waiting and expecting Him to act without our participation. God has invited us to a life with Him where we explore what it means to be truly human in response to His divine grace.

The stories that we have shared are examples of what God has done. At the same time, they are stories of what we have done together, because a life with Christ is an interactive life, where we grow and learn from Him through our actions. Rebecca described that when we were given the Habakkuk text, we made a decision to be intentional and to read, discuss, and pray over it (chapter 8). That was an act of participation with God, even while we were waiting for Him to act. Similarly, when I was in the hiring process with Peachtree, I took time to discuss the possibility with people who knew the church well and could give me their perspectives (chapter 9). Even when we sense God leading, we should use our minds and all of our abilities to participate along with Him.

These experiences we have shared have once again reminded us of the importance of taking time to reflect on our story. A memoir is, by definition, a narrative describing important parts of our lives. We all have a narrative that God is writing with our lives that is just waiting to be explored and re-explored. A critical part of that exploration is experiencing God through the narrative of Scripture. While God guides us through a variety of ways, He will never lead us in conflict with His Word. The foundation of this memoir was God integrating our experiences with the words of the prophet Habakkuk:

> *I will stand at my post,*
> *I will take up my position on the watch-tower,*
> *I will watch to learn what [God] will say through me,*
> *and what I shall reply when I am challenged.*
> *Then the* Lord *made answer:*
> *Write down the vision, inscribe it on tablets,*
> *ready for a herald to carry it with speed;*
> *for there is still a vision for the appointed time.*
> *At the destined hour it will come in* breathless haste,
> *it will not fail.*
> *If it delays, wait for it;*
> *for when it comes will be no time to linger.*
> *The reckless will be unsure of himself,*

Epilogue

> *while the righteous one will live by being faithful . . .*
> —Habakkuk 2:1–4, neb (emphasis added)

While the meaning of those verses are found in their original context and time, God used them to speak to us in our own personal situation. Those words written so long ago give us a picture of how we can find God in our ordinary lives.

Posture

I will stand at my post.

I have an image in my mind of someone standing on a watchtower with arms outstretched and hands open, waiting for a vision from God. I imagine it that way, because our posture while waiting is critical. As I reflect on our story, some of the times when we experienced God in the most dramatic ways was when we said, "Whatever." We will do whatever You want, go wherever You lead, whenever You tell us. It was that posture that led me to sell my business when I first sensed a call to ministry (chapter 3). It was also our posture in those months before leaving the church in Chicago and being led to Peachtree (chapter 9). That is such a hard posture to take, even now. More often than not, we negotiate with God instead of surrendering to God. However, I believe God most often speaks in extraordinary ways to those who take that posture and are prepared to respond to whatever He asks.

I will take up my position on the watch-tower.

We must create space for reflection on what God has done and time to watch for what He might to do in our lives in the time ahead. The verses from Habakkuk paint a picture of someone prepared to actively listen for God's voice. I think that one of the reasons we were able to discern the voice of God was because we had created intentional times of solitude and quiet in our lives. We must relentlessly carve out space to listen. Rebecca described her solitude days dedicated to journaling, walks, and even taking naps as important for hearing from God (chapter 8). I recognized the frozen snow in the crook of a tree, because during that time of my life I was very intentional about taking days of solitude in a remote area to listen for God's voice (chapter 5). I wonder how often I have missed His voice in the rush of my noisy life.

We also must create space to listen to other faithful followers, as He may speak through the wisdom of others. Rebecca was encouraged by a friend to be open to going to Chicago when the two of them took a walk together and Rebecca shared how she had been awakened over and over (chapter 4). I listened to my Algonquin Lakes neighbor who suggested that I read the Mary Oliver poem (chapter 9). We need faithful friends, and we have to find our own watchtower—be it a particular space or time—to hear how God will guide us along our journey.

I will watch to learn what [God] will say through me.

During those years, we lived in a posture of expectation that God was going to act. For that reason, we were always watching for any sign of His activity. It reminds me of walking outside on a dark night. It takes time for your eyes to adjust to the darkness, but soon you begin to see more and more of the stars overhead. We were sensitive to seeing His activity in our lives and in the lives of others. This posture of expectation, always watching with a heightened awareness of the surrounding circumstances, allowed us to connect the dots and recognize His movement. Our story is filled with these types of experiences: a conversation at a McDonald's (chapter 1), sensing God's leading in prayer (chapter 3), the words of a song or poem (chapters 4, 5, and 9). I am sure there are many more that we never recognized, not because God was not speaking, but because we missed them in the hurry and distraction of life.

Write down the vision, inscribe it on tablets.

I can't overstate that without our journals there would be no memoir—no history or dates or details clearly documenting the ways in which we found God in our lives. They provided a record of events and an avenue to seek God's will in our lives. We simply don't have the capacity to remember the small moments in our lives that may have eternal significance. So much of this memoir comes from the pages of our journals. So often our scribbling turned into profound evidence of God's activity. Rebecca's notes about different medical alternatives helped to paint a billboard leading us toward Neale's birth in Michigan (chapter 2). The act of journaling allows us to process events as they are happening. My journals are filled with thoughts and feelings I had as I tried to navigate so much deconstruction in my life (chapter 5). Those written thoughts help me find comfort and lead to clarity in my thinking and feeling. It also allows us to write out our frustrations, our questions, and our prayers as life unfolds and then, in retrospect, to see how they were answered. As we read back through our journals, we see how events that seemed unrelated turned out to be significant, and how God was at work even when we thought Him to be silent. Inscribing our hopes, fears, and desires helps us to clarify our vision and experience God's faithfulness.

Preparation

If it delays, wait for it.

So often on our journey, we thought we were ready to hear from God when, in reality, we were not actually prepared to respond. Waiting on God can be frustrating, but it is also a time of preparation. When we went to Chicago, Rebecca viewed that time as a season of preparation for me through seminary. However, it also was a time of preparation for her as she began to work with her mentor to redeem her story and help others do the same (chapter 6). We must realize that His perspective is far greater than ours, and His timing is, indeed, perfect. As I recounted, I experienced a time of frustration waiting for God. However, at that same time, I also experienced the profound impact of taking a justice journey and a dangerous trip to Malawi. God was using that time of waiting to prepare me for what was to follow (chapter 7). It is important to wait with patience, trusting in God's perfect timing. As the text tells us, it will come at a destined hour, when we are prepared to respond.

For when it comes there will be no time to linger.

As I read these words that describe patient waiting followed by a swift response, I think of a sprinter in the blocks. The runner waits and waits for the gun to go off, coiled and prepared to run down the track. That has been our experience on a number of occasions: waiting followed by frenetic activity. It is critical that during our times of waiting we are preparing ourselves to move in whatever ways God leads. That might mean disconnecting from other commitments or bringing our families into the process (chapters 4 and 8). We often have the misconception that waiting on God means doing nothing. A better way to think about

Epilogue

it is waiting *with* God, because a time of waiting is a time of intentionally seeking him. The things that might hinder us and make us slow to move or stumble out of the blocks should be removed, that way we won't need to linger when the starting gun sounds.

God still does act in our ordinary lives in extraordinary ways, in thousands of acts of grace each and every day. Some are dramatic, even miraculous, and some are small and may even seem mundane. Most of them we miss in the distraction of our lives. However, they are there if only we have ears to hear and eyes to see. We see them by being faithful, but they occur because of His faithfulness.

Our prayer is that our story will encourage you to open up your eyes, ears, heart—and perhaps even a journal—to help you find God's extraordinary presence in your ordinary life in the days ahead so that you, too, can respond with breathless haste.

ACKNOWLEDGEMENTS

First, thank you from the bottom of our hearts to our loving parents, Sara and Lewis Madden and Ed and "Hatsy" Young, who brought us up in faith-filled homes and took us to church, which laid the early foundations of our faith. To Fred Morris, who has supported Sara so tenderly and faithfully so that we could continue in our ministry. To Sara Morris, who encouraged us on our ministry journey during her long illness when she could have asked us to remain nearby. To our children, Brock, Neale, and William, who through their lives have drawn us closer to God and brought us to our knees in prayer. To Rebecca's sisters, Claudia Venable, Harriet Charles, and Virginia Gean, who have cheered, prayed, laughed, cried, and traveled with us all along our winding journey.

To all the pastors, leaders, volunteers, and congregations at Ebenezer Baptist Church and Edwards Road Baptist Church, we thank you for creating a place and space for us to hear God's Word for the first time. Now that we have served on church staffs, we appreciate you more than ever!

To the pastors at First Presbyterian Church and to our dear friends in the Flock Sunday school class who loved us in the hardest season of our lives and helped us to grow in our faith and experience the love of Christ through their actions of prayer, meals, and love. They were the wind beneath our wings. Without them, we would not have a faith story to tell. Thanks for being our lifelong friends!

Breathless Haste

We are so grateful to our friends and the staff of the church in Chicago and Peachtree Presbyterian Church. Thank you for guiding us, believing in us, and challenging us to serve in leadership roles in these amazing churches!

To those who have mentored and encouraged us along our faith journey, we give thanks to Bob Jones, Sheryl Fleisher, Sibyl Towner, Sharon Swing, and Joan Kelley. Thank you also to the Renovaré leaders, teachers, and the two-year cohort Rebecca was able to join.

To our children and our Atlanta friends who turned into book editors. Thank you to Neale Madden, William Madden, Carla Heard, Ryan Jackson, Katherine McCormick, Kathy Ray, and Bill Tucker, who gave of their time, talent, and wisdom to shape this book into its best self. To each of them, cheers and thanks, as we did this memoir of faith together!

We are forever grateful that God pointed us to our professional editor, Heather Campbell! Her story and our story had so many overlapping elements that we were in awe. For hours on end, with all her heart, mind, and soul, she reviewed every word, every phrase, every sentence multiple times. Everything she touched made it the best version it could be.

With a heart of gratitude to those who helped us put the polishing touches on the book. To Miriam Ryan, who used her faith and her love of asking questions to create great ones to help engage our readers. To Vic Lacey, whose incredible photography of Yosemite graces our cover. As he takes his faith-based work around the world, he also takes his camera and captures the grandeur of God's creation.

To Ashley Grandchamp, who shared the hope*books launch announcement that we almost missed—thank you! And to hope*books for your work to encourage writers to share our unique voices. We are so thankful to Brian Dixon, Krissy Nelson, Molly Wilcox, Abby McDonald, Sariah Solomon, and the others on the hope*books professional, innovative, and faith-based team that helped us launch our words into the world. We are so very grateful for your collaboration, knowledge, and depth of experience. We absolutely could not have done this without you—nor would we have wanted to!

And to Jesus, author and perfector of our faith, we thank you for giving your life so that we could have a life filled with love, purpose, joy, and hope.

Printed in the USA
CPSIA information can be obtained
at www.ICGtesting.com
LVHW011100291123
764897LV00042B/200